THE
DIGITAL DIPLOMACY HANDBOOK

How to use social media
to engage with
global audiences

www.digitaldiplomacyhandbook.com

Published in December 2014
Copyright © Antonio Deruda 2014

All rights reserved. No part of this book may be reproduced, stored in a retrieval system, communicated or transmitted in any form or by any means without written permission of the copyright owner.

To my wonderful family,

TABLE OF CONTENTS

INTRODUCTION..................................1

CHAPTER 1 – Social media overview..............5
Definition of social media
Types of social media
How people get news
Main social media trends

CHAPTER 2 - Building your social media roadmap..13
4 steps to developing a social media roadmap
Social media monitoring and listening
Opening accounts and starting to publish content
Enhancing interaction with users
Involving users in decision-making processes
Mixing different levels of engagement

CHAPTER 3 - Setting up a social media monitoring system...................................23
The Social Media Intelligence
Filtering the information flow
What to monitor
Where to listen
Choosing the monitoring tools
How to set up a free social media monitoring system
How to choose advanced monitoring software
Analyzing the monitoring results
Integrating the monitoring activity into your daily job

CHAPTER 4 - Developing your social media strategy..37
7 steps to developing an effective social media strategy
Step 1: Identify your Goals
Step 2: Set Objectives

Step 3: Identify the target audience
Step 4: Allocate a Budget
Step 5: Develop a Content Plan
Trans-creation is better than translation
Think mobile
Step 6: Ensure a smooth workflow
Step 7: Choose the right tools

CHAPTER 5 - Establishing a social media Policy..51
Two kinds of social media policy
The internal social media policy
The external social media policy
Social media policy for specific platforms

CHAPTER 6 – Twitter...............................63
Why use Twitter?
The birth of "Twiplomacy"
Twitter basics
Setting your Twitter profile
What to tweet
How to write good tweets
The power of visuals
How to find people to follow
Building lists
Interacting with users: how to organize a tweetchat
Twitter advertising

CHAPTER 7 – Facebook............................91
5 things to ponder before opening a Facebook page
Setting up a Facebook page
Content strategy
How to write on Facebook
The importance of visual content
Geo-targeting features
Facebook advertising
Managing the conversations

How to promote your page
Measuring your performances

CHAPTER 8 – YouTube...........................113
Why use YouTube?
Setting up a YouTube channel
Recommended format of your videos
Creating good videos
How to make your videos rank better on YouTube
YouTube analytics basics

CHAPTER 9 - Google+ and LinkedIn..........127
Why use Google+?
How to set up a Google+ page
Google+ Circles
5 tips for sharing good content on Google+
Google+ Hangout
Google+ Insights
Why use LinkedIn?
How to create a LinkedIn page
LinkedIn geo-targeting features
LinkedIn groups

CHAPTER 10 – Instagram........................145
Why use Instagram?
How to set up an Instagram account
3 Web apps to enhance Instagram on your desktop
10 tips to get the most out of Instagram

ABOUT THE AUTHOR...........................153

INTRODUCTION

Over the last few years, the term "digital diplomacy" has become a buzzword. Several articles, research papers and surveys have explored how governments and international organizations use the Internet and social media to achieve their strategic goals in foreign policy.

This book is different from any of the material that has been published so far. It is the first practical guide that does not merely talk about digital diplomacy, but explains step-by-step how to do it.

It provides diplomats, international officers, public diplomacy scholars and communications professionals with tactics and tips on how to use social media to engage with global audiences.

Working as a consultant and trainer for government agencies, Foreign Affairs ministries and international organizations, I have developed the belief that diplomatic activity needs to evolve in order to deal with the current international scenario, in which multiple actors - networks of citizens, NGOs, multinational companies, grassroots movements - have the power to influence the decision-making processes, not least through the new communications technologies. "Likes", "Retweets" and "Hashtags" are no longer only for private exchanges among people, but can shape the global agenda.

The disruptive social, political, economic and cultural changes that information networks have unleashed demand a thoughtful rethinking of diplomacy. This does not mean replacing negotiations with exchanges of tweets, but complementing traditional foreign policy methods with new tools that fully leverage the interconnected world in which we all live.

Diplomacy has always had to adapt to changes. This time, however, the challenge is extremely demanding because embracing social media requires governments to review their traditional one-way communication style, build an open dialogue with citizens worldwide and embrace bottom-up ideas. The most valuable aspect of social media is not just the opportunity to reach new audiences and disseminate targeted messages more effectively, but the ability to increase mutual understanding between governments and citizens worldwide.

Tweeting about foreign policy in less than 140 characters, answering questions on Facebook or presenting a video chat on YouTube can be hard to accept for professionals who have historically worked behind closed doors. However, ignoring these tools or thinking that social media is just a passing phenomenon would be a huge mistake. To perform their tasks effectively, diplomats need a deeper understanding of the online platforms that citizens around the world use daily to gather information, consume news, discuss ideas, build relationships and interact with institutions.

This book offers detailed explanations of how to monitor the web, filter relevant information, identify prominent influencers, design global social media strategies, develop compelling content to engage multicultural audiences, manage online conversations and master the main social media channels, such as Facebook, Twitter, YouTube and others.

Ten years ago, this list of skills would have been unfathomable for a diplomat. Today, it simply features the up-to-date basics of good communication. And good communication has always been, and still is, the essence of good diplomacy.

CHAPTER 1
SOCIAL MEDIA OVERVIEW

Definition of social media

Let's start with the basics: what is social media? There is no single and globally recognized definition. According to Wikipedia:

Social media is the social interaction among people in which they create, share or exchange information and ideas in virtual communities and networks.

There are many other definitions of social media. Here are some of the most noteworthy:

Social media is online communications in which individuals shift fluidly and flexibly between the role of audience and author (Joseph Thornley).

Social Media is the democratization of information, transforming people from content readers into publishers. It is the shift from a broadcast mechanism, one-to-many, to a many-to-many model, rooted in conversations between authors, people, and peers (Brian Solis).

Social media describes a variety of Web-based platforms, applications and technologies that enable people to socially interact with one another online (Webopedia).

All the previous definitions contain some keywords that are the cornerstones of the social media world:

- Users
- Networks
- Communities
- Conversations
- Participation
- Engagement
- Interaction
- Content
- Sharing

*Should we treat social media as a singular or a plural noun?
Technically, media is the plural of the Latin term medium and we should therefore use a plural verb. Plus, the term refers to many communication channels, such as Facebook, YouTube, Twitter, etc. But several people claim that the various tools form a new phenomenon or concept in communication and for this reason they treat social media as a singular. This is the reason why if you browse the web or read books about communication and marketing you could find both the plural and singular.

Types of social media

There is often confusion between social media and social networks. The latter belong to the macro group of social media, which according to Andreas Kaplan and Michael Haenle consists of six different types:

- **Collaborative projects** (e.g., Wikipedia)
- **Blogs and microblogs** (e.g., Tumblr and Twitter)
- **Content communities** (e.g., YouTube)

- **Social networks** (e.g., Facebook)
- **Virtual game-worlds** (e.g., World of Warcraft)
- **Virtual social worlds** (e.g. Second Life)

However, the boundaries between these different types have become increasingly blurred.

Another classification of social media includes the following types of tools:

Social networks: online platforms that promote social interaction among users through posts, comments, photos and videos shared among a defined community of contacts or fans (e.g., Facebook, Google+).

Blogs: websites with regular entries such as articles, photos or videos, (e.g., WordPress, Tumblr).

Microblogs: platforms where people share content in a limited message format using status updates, links, photos and videos (e.g.Twitter).

Photo/Video sharing: platforms where users upload, share, view and comment on videos or photos (e.g., Flickr, Instagram for photos; YouTube, Vimeo for video).

Location-based social networks: tools that allow users to check-in and connect with people as they explore a particular place (e.g., Foursquare).

Social news/bookmarking: forums where users share social news trends. (e.g., Reddit, Digg).

Visual bookmarking: platforms that use a "visual" bookmark feature to allow users to share links to information through imagery (e.g., Pinterest).

It's hard to set the borders of the ever-changing world of social media. Since 1994, when Beverly Hills Internet launched Geocities, the first social platform that allowed users to create their own websites modeled after types of urban areas, digital communications tools have dramatically changed our lives. There are plenty of statistics about their growing impact on our societies worldwide.

Official Tumblr page of the Embassy of the United Arab Emirates in Washington

How people get news
For the purpose of this book it is noteworthy to emphasize how social media is changing the way people get, share and discuss news.

According to a Pew Research Center study issued at the end of 2013, 50% of the US public cites the Internet as a main source for national and international news, up from 43% in 2011. Television (69%) remains the public's top source for news. Far fewer cite newspapers (28%) or radio (23%) as their main source. The importance of the web is guaranteed to increase in the near future, since 71% of young people (18-29) cite the Internet as a main news source, more than the percentage that cites television.

The current media landscape is starkly different to that of 2001, when 45% said newspapers were their main source for news and just 13% cited the Internet. Another significant statistic cited in the study says that 65% of those who consider the Internet a main news source say traditional news organizations are politically biased, while 73% say that they spend too much time on unimportant stories and 81% say they are often influenced by powerful people and their reports are not fair.

The role of Internet and social media in the way people get news in the US is dramatically increasing and the same is happening worldwide, with different intensity and pace depending on the culture and the level of web penetration.

The trend towards a future central role of social platforms in the media landscape seems well consolidated. Governments and international organizations that want to inform and influence people cannot ignore social media anymore and should closely follow how these tools, and the way people use them, are evolving.

The Instagram account of the Israeli Foreign Affairs Ministry

Main social media trends
- Brands and organizations as media companies
Social media has given innovative businesses, organizations and even governments the power to become publishers and to directly reach a wide public. Creating valuable content and sharing it on social platforms is an effective way to stir global conversations and engage the target audience.

- Visual content is king
The rapid market penetration of smartphones and tablets, the availability of high speed wireless networks and other factors have prompted the emergence of focused visual media social networks such as Pinterest, Instagram, Vine and others. Even on platforms like Facebook, Twitter or Tumblr, imagery is now predominant.

- Optimizing content for mobile is mandatory
A couple of years ago it was good to have a mobile content strategy. Now it has become mandatory. The rise of mobile devices worldwide means that optimizing the social content for mobile is a vital step, as we will see in the chapter on how to build a social media strategy.

- The increasing authority of online influencers
Over the last years online influencers in their niches have grown large and relevant communities of followers. Establishing and cultivating relationships with these influencers through an effective activity of online PR is crucial to achieve the organization's strategic goals.

- Social media is not free
Paying to reach the target audience on Facebook has become the norm (we will analyze the limit of Facebook organic reach in chapter 7). Twitter, LinkedIn and Pinterest have also developed advertising schemes similar to Facebook. The assumption that "with social media we can reach an unlimited global audience almost for free" is definitively over.

- **Social listening is crucial**
More businesses are beginning to really listen to their customers. Some governments are doing the same by monitoring online conversations in order to analyze public opinion and understand how to influence the opinion-making process at local and global level. Social media monitoring and listening to online conversations is the first essential step in order to develop an effective social media strategy (see Chapter 3).

We must not make the mistake of thinking that social media is a passing phenomenon. While it is difficult to predict whether in the next years the current major social platforms will be able to keep the leadership of the market, it is well established that these tools have created a new way of working and building relations doomed to last a long time.

CHAPTER 2
BUILDING YOUR SOCIAL MEDIA ROADMAP

4 steps to develop a social media roadmap

Shifting from a top-down, one-way communication approach to a strategy that uses the web and social media as two-way communication channels implies for governments and organizations a thoughtful assessment of the kind of social media presence they are able to establish based on various elements (political and cultural practices, human resources, available skills, budget, etc.).

It is not true, as many believe, that getting into social media immediately involves a high degree of engagement. Governments, diplomatic missions or international organizations might find it helpful to follow a 4-step path that gradually leads to the full maturity of their social media presence:

1) Monitoring social media and listening to online conversations
2) Opening accounts on different platforms and starting to publish valuable content
3) Stimulating interactions and actively participating in conversations
4) Involving citizens in decision-making processes through social media

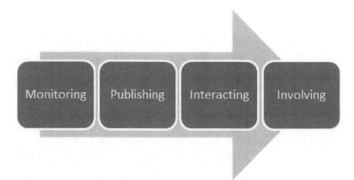

The social media roadmap

Social media monitoring and listening

Opening an official Facebook page, a Twitter account or a YouTube channel is usually the first step an organization takes when it believes the time has come to use social media.

However, this could be a big mistake. Using different social channels implies having to know the rules, the kind of users and how they interact, the quality and the characteristics of the most shared content and so on. Before establishing a social media presence, it is therefore essential to gather all the information needed to successfully manage these multifaceted platforms.

A diplomatic mission, for example, might decide not to join any social media, due to lack of human resources or budget restraints.
But it would be a very bad decision not to monitor social media and ignore what the local citizens think about the government's political moves or about the strategic topics that the mission has to cover.

As the first step into the social media environment, it is helpful and crucial to set up a listening and monitoring activity that can later lead to the second step: opening the accounts and starting to publish content. Social media monitoring and listening is often overlooked, but in reality it is so important that it deserves a separate chapter of this book.

Opening accounts and starting to publish content

A first and basic practice is to open one or more accounts on social media and start publishing content. At the time of Web 1.0 businesses and organizations used to publish information on their website, trying to drive traffic there. Nowadays the challenge is to convey content and messages in those virtual places where citizens get news, discuss, share content, and build relations. That does not mean ignoring the institutional website, which, indeed, keeps a central role because it should be the point of reference to which users should be directed to in order to provide more in-depth content.

Opening an account requires organization, method and established skills. Using social media does not mean, as many still assume, copying and pasting press releases on Facebook, but it implies setting up a smooth internal workflow, clearly identifying tasks and processes, using different languages and styles based on the platforms, transforming a long report in 3-4 tweets, filming and editing a short video of an event or managing bad comments, just to name some of the required skills.

The practice shows that today many diplomatic missions or other international organizations open up accounts on social media skipping the fundamental monitoring and listening phase and without the proper preparation that even the most basic level of social media presence requires.

Last year, a sarcastic article published by popular online media Buzzfeed reported nine cases of foreign embassies in Washington that gave up their Twitter adventure after a bunch of tweets. It's the typical outcome when organizations join social media without the proper planning, just because everybody is using it.

Enhancing interaction with users

Social media users are familiar with the inner nature of these tools, which is based on interaction and sharing. Therefore, using these tools like a microphone might end up being counterproductive for an organization.

Today, by opening an account on Twitter or Facebook we announce to users that we are ready to talk to them, to answer their questions and to accept criticisms and suggestions. Ignoring these expectations can have a negative impact on the reputation of the diplomats as well as of the governments or organizations they represent.

Ensuring a good level of interaction through social media is definitely a strong commitment a diplomatic mission must undertake. It also represents an important opportunity because a straight relationship based on mutual trust can be of great value to better convey the messages, to explain the political views, or, more generally, to promote the image of the country. Surely, users will be more willing to accept messages from a source that is ready to discuss or accept different views.

Creating an interactive relationship with the online community is also useful for diplomats in order to get information and valuable feedback for one of their main tasks: the political and social analysis.

In the previous step - opening an account – an organization merely publishes content and answers questions or responds to comments in a rather passive way. At this stage, instead, the organization has to stimulate dialogue, participate in conversations and offer opportunities for exchange with users, such as Q&A sessions or live-chats.

A great example is the decision of British FA Minister William Hague to mark his 200,000th follower on Twitter by asking users to tweet the answer to this question: "What do you think is the biggest contribution UK foreign policy can make to the world?" The winning entry was from Gopal Rao, an Indian student at the University of Cambridge, who answered: "UK foreign policy should focus on emancipation of #girlsandwomen through enterprise, supported by vibrant #socent culture within UK". Hague then invited the student to the Foreign Office for a meeting where they discussed the "Preventing Sexual Violence in Conflict" initiative.

The Foreign Office website reporting about the meeting between William Hague and Gopal Rao

This level of social media presence is valuable and offers great opportunities to improve the reputation of a country or organization, but it is also challenging: it implies a fluid workflow to manage the comments, a streamlined chain of command to quickly approve the answers to users, an adequate preparation to handle any crisis communication and more time and resources to devote to social media.

Involving users in decision-making processes

The last step involves the highest level of engagement and is associated to innovative methods such as online consultations or participation of citizens in different phases of the decision-making process.

So far, governments' foreign policy decisions haven't been largely affected by the major trend that sees citizens playing an increasing role in various decision-making processes at local, national and partly global levels. However, over the last few years some foreign ministries and international organizations have carried out attempts to stimulate citizens' participation in different ways. For instance, when in 2012 the British Foreign Office started the process to review its communication strategy, it asked users on social media to submit suggestions and comments, on the assumption that thanks to the web it is possible to get ideas and advice that can enhance the government's action in the international arena.

Promoting citizens' participation through the web is the most advanced and challenging use of social media. Not all governments and organizations are ready to undertake this step, which implies an open approach, full transparency, the ability to filter and manage the external inputs and a real willingness to include the citizens' proposals in the formulation of policies. This level also requires a cultural change in the whole organization: recognizing the deep change of the relationship with citizens, who are not only a target of the institutional communication, but can be strategic partners in the policy-making process.

Mixing different levels of engagement
In a social media strategy that includes different tools or multiple accounts on the same platform, it might be good to establish different levels of engagement.

Again, British diplomacy offers an interesting example to analyze. The embassy in Lebanon has two Twitter accounts: one of the mission and another one of the ambassador. The account of the mission has a more formal tone; it mostly features information on the institutional activity and has little interaction with users. The account of Ambassador Tom Fletcher, considered a major digital diplomacy champion, is more informal, there are casual conversations with some followers, as well as selfies, jokes and comments that sometimes are not in line with the formal language of diplomacy.

The embassy account has about 8,000 followers. Tom Fletcher has 32,000. These numbers confirm that social media users generally prefer the personal profiles rather than the institutional ones and they appreciate officials that are not afraid of showing their human side.

The two accounts integrate seamlessly with each other by exchanging continuous retweets in order to maximize the reach of the messages.

The mission's social media presence also includes accounts on Flickr and YouTube, and a Facebook page with about 9,000 Likes. Here the social media managers try to engage users with "soft" content: topics close to young people, such as education and scholarships, numerous photos and regular Q&A sessions on various subjects.

The Twitter account of the British Embassy to Lebanon

When a diplomatic mission can rely both on its own social media accounts and on those of the ambassador, it is essential to create a solid integration between these accounts. In particular, the ambassador should invite his contacts to also follow the institutional profile and should share almost all messages published by the embassy. The major reason is that the network of local followers or fans that a diplomat can create is destined to disappear when he leaves the post and moves to another country. It is therefore necessary to focus on developing and securing the audience of the embassy's social media channels.

CHAPTER 3
SETTING UP A SOCIAL MEDIA MONITORING SYSTEM

The Social Media Intelligence

As we saw in the previous chapter, before establishing a social media presence it is essential to monitor the web and the online conversations. This is where all digital projects should begin: with focused monitoring rather than unfocused publishing.

The importance assumed by online monitoring has given birth to a new discipline, the so-called Social Media Intelligence, a methodology that helps to make decisions and establish strategies through the analysis of data and information from social platforms. This is not only in business, but in politics and diplomacy as well.

One of the most important activities of a diplomat has historically been to collect and analyze information on the political, social, economic and cultural environment of the country in which he operates. Today, this task could not be accurately performed without considering social media and its impact in shaping the public opinion.

The traditional primary sources of information (the diplomats' network of contacts in the political, business, media and social environment) and the secondary sources (such as public data or press articles) can be supported by social media intelligence, through which it is possible to identify new opinion makers and examine their conversations in the virtual platforms. Social media tools cannot entirely displace established methods of intelligence gathering, but they should be used as a helpful complementary tool.

Filtering the information flow
Recently, the number of websites on the Internet has exceeded one billion worldwide. This is what happens online every second:
- Around 8,000 tweets are sent on Twitter
- 1,400 photos are posted on Instagram
- 5,000 status updates and 136,000 photos are uploaded on Facebook
- 90,000 videos are seen on YouTube
- 1,500 blog posts are published on Tumblr
- Over 45,000 searches on Google

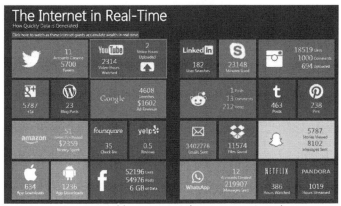

Source: http://pennystocks.la/internet-in-real-time/

How is it possible to monitor such a huge and multidimensional online universe?

As the Internet and the amount of information it provides continue to expand, the decision-making processes are becoming increasingly tough. The aim is to find tools that allow filtering and organizing the overwhelming information flow.

Diplomats and international officers have two main challenges. One is to find all the relevant information online and bring it back in such a way that it is possible to make the best use of it. The other challenge is the time factor: it is necessary to organize a monitoring system that allows filtering the information in a very short time.

Here's 5-step guide to help you build a social media monitoring activity.

1) What to monitor?

The first step is to know what's worthwhile to monitor and what types of searches will net you the best results. It is important to choose the right keywords and continuously refine them because even the most accurate search will generate irrelevant results. Only a clean stock of search results can make this activity useful.

Choosing keywords is one of the most important decisions to make. Picking broad terms will flood you with irrelevant results and give you the laborious task of weeding through thousands of unnecessary content. Going too narrow – or too technical – will severely limit your results.

2) Where to listen

After deciding on the keywords, it's time to locate the websites, blogs, forums, social networks or other platforms where conversations relevant to your activity take place. You can start by including the main sources (newspapers, magazines, online media, blogs, key influencers on Twitter, etc.). The analysis of the results will allow the discovery new sources that are relevant to your activity and objectives.

The selection of sources is a tough task. According to Seth Grimes, an authority on text mining, source selection criteria include:

Topicality: it is a judgment that the source contains the information you need and enough of that information to justify mining it.

Focus: when the source contains a high proportion of relevant information.

Currency: it is the timeliness of information, a measure of whether, for a particular task, the information is out of date. Nowadays items that are even a few hours old may be little more than noise.

Authority: it is the trustworthiness of an information source.

3) Choosing the monitoring tools

The web and social media monitoring market is a crowded one. There are many different types of tools, i.e. enterprise ones, research ones, engagement ones or basic ones. I often suggest to begin the monitoring and listening activity using free tools for three main reasons. The first is that I am well aware that public organizations around the world have to deal with budget constraints and it is difficult to get a lot of money for this type of activity. The second reason is that in the initial phase, when you start learning how to monitor, it would be difficult to manage complex software. Finally, in recent years the free tools have achieved good levels that may be sufficient for the type of monitoring that a single diplomatic mission or small international organizations have to perform.

How to set up a free social media monitoring system

There are tons of free online monitoring tools you can explore and test. I think the following ones can be a good starting point:

Google Alerts
Google has a service that notifies you via email when the search engine finds new results, web pages, newspaper articles or blogs that match your selected search terms or phrases.

How to create an alert:
Visit Google Alerts and enter in the words you want to get email notifications for in the "Create an alert about" box.

Click "Show options" to customize the alerts:

How often: to help manage your inbox, choose how often you want to get notified.

Sources: if you only want to see results from a specific source, you can choose it here. The automatic option, which provides you with the best results from multiple sources, is advisable.

Language: you'll get alerts for search results in the language you select.

Region: if you only want to see results from or related to a particular country or region, you can select it here.

How many: only the best results or all results.

Deliver to: choose an email to send alerts to.

Click Create Alert.

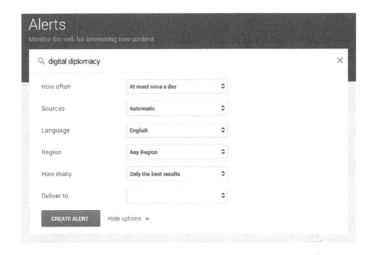

Once your alert is set up, you'll start getting emails anytime Google finds new search results for your keywords.

Google suggests the following tips for creating alerts:
- Try to be as precise as possible. The more precise your search terms are, the more relevant your alerts will be.
- Use quotes around a group of words if you are looking for them together. For example: "White house".
- Use a minus sign (-) in front of words that you want to exclude. For example: [paris -hilton].
- Use the "site: operator" to limit your search to specific sites.

RSS Reader
Subscribing to a website RSS through an RSS Reader removes the need to manually check websites for new content.

The Reader constantly monitors the web and informs the user of any updates. How RSS technically works is not important. The key point here is that it allows for having online sources of your choice deliver their latest news directly to your pc or mobile device. So you can use a single tool to monitor different websites and see all the information aggregated into a single dashboard and divided in topics you can customize.

After the closure of Google Reader in 2013, one of the most popular and free RSS Readers is Feedly, but there are other free platforms you can test.

Netvibes
You can use Netvibes to create several so-called dashboards, dynamic workspaces to gather all the content that's relevant to you, by adding modules called widgets, which provide specific information or functionality. Netvibes is useful to monitor everything about a topic on the web and on social networks, all in one place. It also includes an RSS Reader where you can add content from all your favorite websites. Netvibes also makes it easy to share content from your dashboard: with just a click, you can share an article on Twitter, Facebook and other platforms.

Topsy.com
Topsy.com is a free real-time search engine that permits to search by time and place, set alerts, and analyze sentiment for every tweet ever sent since 2006. The tool also ranks results using a proprietary social influence algorithm that measures the "social media influence" of the users.

Topsy is useful for identifying the community of Twitter users talking about topics you have decided to monitor.

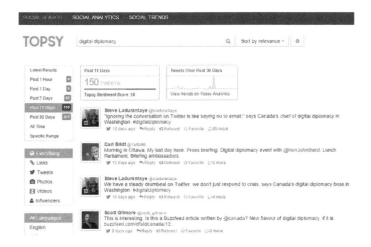

Social Mention
Social Mention is a social media search and analysis platform that aggregates content from the web into a single stream of information. It allows you to track and measure what people are saying about any topic across the social media landscape in real-time.

Twitter
With Twitter alone, there are a ton of ways to get insights and intelligence. Here are a few ideas. We will go more in-depth in Chapter 6, which is dedicated to the most popular micro-blogging platform.

- Create and save Twitter searches focusing on major terms and hashtags related to your activity.

- Monitor hashtags for discussions or events related to your activity.

- Create Twitter lists of major influencers and news sources in your fields.
- Create Twitter lists focusing on specific topics.
- Monitor conversations on topics of your interest for questions or potential ideas.

How to choose an advanced monitoring software

With the tools highlighted in the previous section you can set up a basic social media monitoring system. But the old adage "you get what you pay for" holds true. If you have a budget, you can choose more advanced software, such as Radian6, Sysomos, and Viralheat, just to name the most popular.

Be aware that some social networks have strict rules that mean it's impossible for tools, even the most advanced and expensive ones, to cover all of the content (i.e. Facebook pages with privacy settings set to private, Facebook messages, protected tweets, Twitter DMs, private messages on forums and so on).

Here is a reworked version of a comprehensive list of the main factors to consider in selecting advanced social media tools (shared by marketing consultant Mauricio Escobar Mármol):

Content - How and with what frequency is the content aggregated? What kind of social media conversations can't the tool monitor? Can the tool track conversations happening in specific areas or in different languages?

Sentiment analysis - Does the tool offer sentiment analysis? What's the algorithm? Can your team be alerted when social media conversations from key influencers bring some sort of "bad sentiment" about your organization?

Data retrieval - How long is content archived? Is back data available? If so, what is the extra cost?

Search results speed - This is key because it affects the speed of your reaction. Ask for a test before signing up.

Dashboard - What dashboard features are available in the standard tool version? Can dashboards be customized by users?

Engagement - social media response What workflow capabilities does the tool offer? Can "owned" content (i.e. your Facebook page or Twitter account) be managed through the monitoring tool?

Integration - What additional types of data can be integrated in the system (i.e. Google Analytics, Email database, etc.)?

Reporting capabilities - Does the standard version allow for reports to be generated?

Pricing structure - There are three main keys for the pricing structure that most Social Media Monitoring tools offer: volume based pricing, search based pricing and a flat rate.

Tool set up - Is there any specific system requirement needed? You might want to check with your IT department to see if there are no issues with installing the tool in your computers. Is training included?

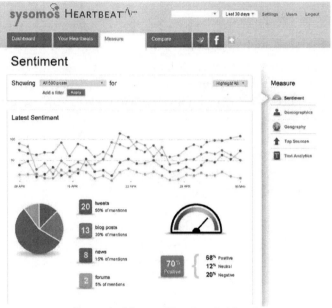

Example of Sysomos Heartbeat dashboard

4) Analyzing the monitoring results
These are some key insights the monitoring activity performed by a diplomatic mission might produce:

Audience: you can discover what they like, what channels they mostly use, when they are there and how they interact.

Sentiment: are people saying mostly positive or mostly negative things about you, your government or your country?

Feedback: Is feedback on the services you provide, such as consular services, good? What can you do to improve them based on the users' opinions?

Questions: Are you seeing frequent questions about your diplomatic activity or your government's political stances? Maybe there's an opportunity to create content that can help answer these questions.

Content: Social media monitoring is a great way to find valuable content you can share with your audience, learn from or build upon with your own creativity.

Public Opinion: Social media doesn't necessarily reflect public opinion, but monitoring online conversations might give useful insights about the public's views on topics that are relevant to your activity.

Advocates: You could discover advocates who talk about you and spread the word about your initiatives. You can use social media to nurture this community of advocates.

Press opportunities: Journalists are increasingly using social media. The monitoring activity can help you get a read on what journalists in your field are working on, what questions they have that you can answer and what they like and dislike when it comes to being pitched.

Influencers: Close monitoring could help you discover someone in your field whose voice resonates a little louder than most.

5) Integrating the monitoring activity in your daily job

Once you have built a monitoring system that meets your needs and your budget, you have to add it in the daily work of the entire organization. For instance, the morning press briefing might also include news and views from various online sources: a blogger or a Twitter user may have more influence power than a traditional newspaper, as well as a wider reach.

Monitoring results should not remain the exclusive use of the communication department, but should be disseminated within the organization through good and brief reporting. Every office can benefit from the results of the monitoring activity. The monitoring system should in particular support all the PR and outreach programs. If, for example, an embassy organizes a conference, online monitoring can help identify the right people to involve, learn more about the speakers you are going to invite, find advocates who can help promote the event, get more insights on the subject of the conference, and anticipate possible questions or criticisms that can be addressed to the mission representatives. During the conference it would be advisable to monitor in real time any online discussions on the subject and soon after the event it's possible to see whether the ideas and messages that emerged had any follow-up in online conversations.

CHAPTER 4
DEVELOPING YOUR SOCIAL MEDIA STRATEGY

7 steps to develop an effective social media strategy

The social media strategy is a plan of action, based on a defined budget, to achieve specific goals by identifying measurable objectives, the target audience, the kind of content to share and the most effective tools to use.

Too often I have seen businesses and organizations building their social media presence by publishing content on some platform without any kind of strategic thinking. Confusing strategy with tactics (the set of means by which a strategy may be the carried out) is a serious mistake.

Before exploring how to build a strategy it is helpful to remember the importance of activating a web and social media monitoring activity, which allows us to identify and better understand the target audience, the best platforms to convey our messages, the type of conversations that take place on our relevant topics, the most searched and appreciated content. Monitoring also allows making a sort of competitors assessment, which means studying the way in which similar organizations communicate with their audience.

Once a wide-ranging monitoring activity is performed, it is possible to start designing the social media strategy by following these seven key steps:

Step 1 - Identify your Goals
Look closely at your organization's overall goals and decide if and how social media can contribute to reach them. Every piece of your social media strategy must serve the strategic goals of your organization. Don't open a Facebook page just because everybody is using it. Think if Facebook is the right platform to achieve one or more goals of your diplomatic mission (i.e. promoting the country as a new tourist destination, attract foreign investments, etc).

The Facebook page of the French Foreign Affairs Ministry

Step 2 - Set Objectives

The words Goal and Objective are often confused with each other. Both terms imply the target that one's efforts is desired to accomplish. Goals are broader than objectives in the sense that they are general intentions and are not specific enough to be measured. An objective has a similar definition but is supposed to be a clear and measurable target.

Goals are not useful if you don't have specific parameters that define when each is achieved. You can use the SMART approach by making your objectives Specific, Measurable, Achievable, Relevant and Time-bound.

An example from the business sector might clear the difference:
Goal: increase our product's share of the market
Objective: increase our product's share of the market by 15% by the end of the next financial year.

Step 3 - Identify the target audience

Online marketers use so-called "personas," fictional characters created to represent the different types of users that might visit a website or interact in a social network. Personas are valuable in considering expectations and habits of online users in order to guide decisions about the visual design of a website or the kind of content to share on social media.

Personas are said to be cognitively compelling because they put a personal human face on otherwise abstract data about online users. With personas, organizations can be more strategic in internalizing the audience that they are trying to attract and relate to them as human beings. Here is a quick overview of what a persona template might include:

- Fictional name
- Age
- Gender
- Language
- Location: urban / suburban / rural
- Education
- Job
- Professional interests
- Hobbies
- Preferred online sources
- Preferred social media
- Kind of information he/she looks for online

Diplomatic missions or international organizations are not companies. Their needs and goals are different. So it is not essential to create elaborated marketing personas (with information about income, purchasing attitude, etc.), but imagining the target audience as a group of real human beings could be a useful brainstorming in order to craft a better online content strategy.

Step 4 - Allocate Budget

I usually advise establishing the budget first and then selecting which tactics fit that budget. Some take the opposite approach: establish a comprehensive strategy first, and then determine the budget that fits it. I think the latter method could be a waste of time, especially in government organizations, where resources for online communications are generally limited. You can design a great social media strategy with a lot of creative ideas and dozens of tools to use and then, when you finally address the budget issue, you suddenly realize that your strategy was just an unrealistic project, a dream that will never come true.

So, it's better to start with an estimated budget that allows to make a comprehensive list of tools and services you can afford (e.g., social media monitoring, graphic design or video production, copywriting, translations) and any advertising you might be able to purchase. Setting up an effective social media presence, building a community and engaging it takes time. For this reason I usually suggest to prepare a 1-year budget plan.

Step 5 - Develop a Content Plan

Content and social media have a symbiotic relationship: without great content, social media is meaningless and without social media nobody will know about your content.

The type of content you should post on each social network relies on form and context. Form is how you present that information: text only, images, video, infographics, etc. Context fits with your organization's voice and the different personalities of the various social media channels.

Your content could be serious or funny, highly technical or tailored for the general public. The choice strongly depends on the social channels you are using. An embassy's economic program, for instance, could be promoted by sharing 1) a detailed document on LinkedIn, 2) a straightforward infographic on Twitter, 3) a story with images on Facebook, 4) a video interview on YouTube, 5) a presentation on Slideshare.

Tailoring the content is one of the most difficult challenges for those working with social media. Copying and pasting a press release on Facebook or posting a 3-hour video of a conference on YouTube is just a waste of time and resources. For this reason, the strategy must include a content audit to see if the information that the organization normally produces can be used on social media. Then it is fundamental to identify who can adapt this content, and how, in order to match the expectations of the target audience.

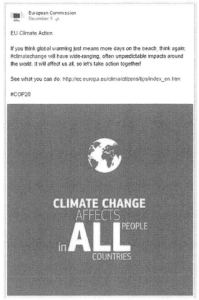

A post in the EU Commission's Facebook page

Organizations must adopt platform-specific personalities and then adapt both their strategy and content to fit those platforms. That's the kind of approach that will enable organizations to engage with audiences. It is crucial to replace the one-size-fits-all mentality with a more nimble approach in which separate audiences are engaged with the same messages but told in different ways. What might work on Twitter may lack the necessary gravitas needed for LinkedIn.

When designing this flexible content strategy, you should consider two other key elements: the language of your information and the devices people will mainly use to consume your content.

Trans-creation is better than translation

Depending on your goals, your target audience, the budget and the human resources available, one of your first decisions will be about the languages of your content. This is a critical aspect for all organizations working in the international relations field.

The golden rule is to use, as much as possible, the language of your target audience. Social media is based on conversations. Consequently, it is important to facilitate interaction with your community.

A diplomatic mission, for instance, might have as target audiences the citizens of the country where it is based, as well as its own nationals. In this case it is important to prepare two separate content plans, because the relevant information for the two publics will be very different. There may be some topics in common, but the simple translation might not be enough, because it is necessary to take into account all the cultural nuances.

Even the most accurate translation cannot have the same effect as content written from scratch in the local language. This is why you should "trans-create" your content rather than just translate it. A trans-creation is content adapted to the local culture. It goes further than using the right phrases; it requires vast local knowledge. In order to make the trans-creation process effective, a diplomatic mission must be ready to give its local employees more creative freedom.

Simply translating words doesn't mean you're providing the right context in a region. And the same goes for photos and videos. There are several challenges, including the following:

- The meaning of a color varies across cultures. In western countries white is associated with purity and the joy of the wedding. In many Asian countries, white is the color of mourning and funerals. Even in the same region the meaning of colors might be extremely different: in all the European countries pink is a feminine color, except in Belgium where pink has traditionally been the color for boys.

- Images of people can be very engaging to convey your message, but they are not appropriate in some cultures, where images of women or of some parts of the human body are not acceptable.

- Visual metaphors or puns may not work in translation. For example, the idea of an owl is a symbol of wisdom in the United States and parts of Europe. But in other cultures, owls are associated with death.

Think mobile

71% of social media users access social networks from a mobile device. That's nearly three out of every four people, according to a recent consumer survey from Adobe. Facebook and Twitter's official statistics confirm this study: 76% of active Twitter users access via a mobile device; of its 1.3 billion monthly active users, Facebook reports that 1.1 billion access the site on a phone or tablet.

Mobile devices are quickly becoming the preferred method of reading, sharing, and engaging with online content. We must consider that what we create on desktops and laptops will end up on dozens of different screen sizes and will likely be consumed in the palm of people's hands.

Your strategy must keep in mind this trend. Here are some tips to develop the right mobile-optimized content plan:

- **Embrace the mobile-first approach:** the current trend says that good web design is mobile-first. The same kind of thinking needs to be applied to how we create content. Thriving in the mobile world requires an increasingly forward-looking approach.

- Use insights to **understand your audience's mobile habits**: what percentage of your audience accesses your site or your social platform on mobile devices? What content are they accessing and sharing most?

- **Focus on headlines and the first two paragraphs**: your headline must be highly relevant to your audience and immediately show the benefit to the reader. The challenge is to offer the key takeaways that people can read in a few seconds of casual mobile browsing.

- **Mix up your content lengths:** try to vary the lengths of the content that you create by highlighting short summaries (in a Facebook post, for instance) and then offering the chance to click over to longer and in-depth articles. If possible always prepare two versions of every piece of content: the long version and the quick hits.

- **Consider a lower level of attention:** keep in mind that people might consume your content while commuting or watching TV. So, be succinct, clear and get straight to the point using plain language.

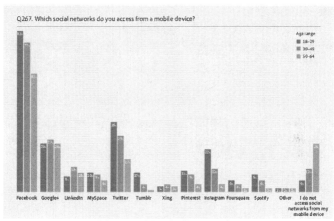

Adobe 2013 Mobile Consumer Survey

Step 6 - Ensure a smooth workflow

Integrating the social media goals with those of your organization, setting specific and realistic targets, finding the right audience and developing an effective content plan can be useless if you don't set up a flexible internal workflow and a smooth chain of command.

This is a tough challenge for all organizations and businesses, especially for governments or diplomatic organizations.

A popular quote says that organizations and businesses need to "be social" and not "do social".

Social media requires a dramatic cultural change that does not only affect the way an organization communicates with the public, but also its internal rules, hierarchies and workflows. Social media is not just something up to the communication department, but the process of creating good content or interacting with online users should involve many other departments.

Before implementing the social media strategy, it is fundamental to answer the following questions that can help you ensure a smooth internal workflow:

- Who within your organization will supervise the social media activity?
- Who will be responsible for content creation?
- How will the different departments of your organization submit content to be shared on social channels?
- What's the approval process of the content?
- Who will manage the online conversations?
- What's the approval process to reply to users? How can this process be circumvented in case of a communication crisis?
- How will the social media main analytics be spread across the organization?

If you don't have the budget to hire a social media manager or an external consultant, avoid the big mistake of giving the responsibility of social media activity to a geek colleague who, "knows perfectly how Facebook and Twitter work," or, even worse, to a "smart intern who is a digital native and spends hours on social media".

Just because someone knows what a hashtag is or how to post a picture on Facebook, it does not mean that he is qualified to choose valuable content for the target audience, manage a community or respond to harsh criticisms. This job requires expertise and training. Unqualified people who manage your social media accounts might cause huge harm to the reputation of your organization.

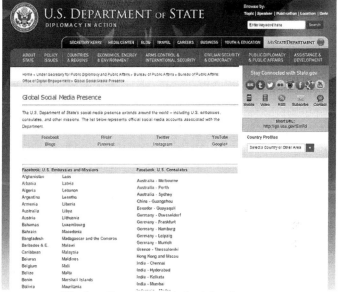

The State Department global social media presence

Step 7 - Choose the right tools
Now that you know your goals, objectives, audience, budget and kind of content you are able to produce, you are ready to choose the right tools.

Most organizations and businesses still approach social media by skipping all the previous steps and start by opening accounts on several platforms.

If, for instance, you are aware that your organization is not be able to create visual content or that you don't have a budget for small advertising campaigns, creating a Facebook page will likely be useless, even if your target audience uses this social platform. Without an advertising budget you will be able to reach very few people and even those who find your page will be unlikely to Like it if you only post press releases or official statements.

There are hundreds of social media platforms available today. Every month new platforms come out and others disappear. Because of the rapid and unpredictable rise of these tools, it is impossible to confine them all in this book. In the next chapters I have decided to focus on the most recognizable social media used by governments and diplomats worldwide.

CHAPTER 5
ESTABLISHING A SOCIAL MEDIA POLICY

Two kinds of social media policy

Using two-way communication channels such as social media poses significant challenges to international organizations. These tools are in fact more complex to handle than the traditional one-way communication channels.

In order to guide the whole organization through the social media environment it is essential to make clear rules and guidelines to your employees as well as to the potential audience that will likely interact with the organization. To achieve this goal, two different documents are required.

1) The internal social media policy: it aims to explain to the employees what tools the organization is using and should make clear functions and rules of the social media management.

2) The external social media policy: it aims to communicate to the public how the organization is using social media and what the rules are that everybody must respect in terms of language, topics, content, copyright issues and so on.

The Internal social media policy

Developing an internal social media policy may raise a range of issues involving many different parts of an organization, including PR, human resources, legal and ICT security areas.

The document can be split into two sections:
1) The first section should answer the following basic questions:
- What are the social media channels?
- Why are they important for the organization?
- Who is in charge of developing and executing the social media strategy?
- Where does the organization share content and engage with the public?

This is how the social media policy of the British Foreign Office begins:

Context: why social media matters
The FCO encourages all staff to make full use of the opportunities offered by social media to help deliver FCO objectives. Social media:
Allows diplomats to monitor events, harvest information and identify key influencers.
Can assist in the consultation process and the formulation of policy by helping us crowd source ideas.
Provide real time channels to deliver our messages directly and influence beyond traditional audiences.
Improve the delivery of our services through closer engagement with our customers and allow us to better manage a crisis.
Make us more accountable and transparent through open dialogue.

The importance of embedding digital tools in policy making and service delivery is set out in more detail in the FCO Digital Strategy.

The Digital Diplomacy website of the Foreign Office

It would also be advisable to point out the code of conduct of the organization when managing the relationship with the community of online users. Here is an interesting excerpt of the U.S. State of Delaware social media policy:

A summary of the key points of ethical Social Media
conduct are reproduced below:
i. Customer protection and respect are paramount.
ii. We will use every effort to keep our interactions
factual and accurate.
iii. We will strive for transparency and openness in our

interactions and will never seek to "spin" information for our benefit.
iv. We will provide links to credible sources of information to support our interactions, when possible.
v. We will publicly correct any information we have communicated that is later found to be in error.
vi. We are honest about our relationship, opinions, and identity.
vii. We respect the rules of the venue.
viii. We protect privacy and permissions.

2) The second section should include guidelines for the employees. Recognizing the different reasons employees engage in social media use and how they sometimes overlap is valuable in creating a good social media policy. There are basically three distinct ways employees can use social media tools:

Employee use for official agency interests: the employee's use of social media is for the express purpose of communicating a government's interests. For example, a diplomat might be asked to report his working experience by writing an article on the diplomatic mission's official blog or Facebook page.

Employee use for professional interests: professional use implies that an employee's use of social media is for the purpose of furthering specific job responsibilities or professional duties. For example, the economic officer of a diplomatic mission might join a LinkedIn group to connect with the local business community or might use Twitter to get news and information relevant to his activity.

Employee use for personal interests: using social media for personal interests has nothing to do with an employee's job duties, but when posting in a personal capacity the employee may still be easily identified as working for an organization.

The boundary between private and professional use of social media is liquid. A diplomatic officer might use his Twitter account to share photos of his vacation as well as to promote an embassy's initiative or to answer questions about visas. There's nothing wrong with it, but the officer should know what he can share, how to write it or how to respond to possible criticisms. For this reason the internal social media policy should not be just a list of "do not", but a real guide to help employees carefully use these tools.

A good example of helpful guidelines is this list of 16 tips from the U.S. Air force:

1) No classified information
Don't post classified, sensitive or For Official Use Only information

2) Stay in your lane
Discussing issues related to your career field or personal experiences are acceptable and encouraged, but you shouldn't discuss areas of expertise where you have no firsthand, direct experience or knowledge.

3) Obey applicable laws
You must keep federal law, Department of Defense directives and instructions in mind when using social media in official and unofficial capacities.

4) Differentiate between opinion and official information
Yes, tell them what you think…just make sure you state that this is your opinion and not that of the organization.

5) Use your best judgment
What you write may have serious consequences. Once you post something on social media, you can't "get it back." Even deleting the post doesn't mean it's truly gone. Ultimately, you bear sole responsibility for what you post.

6) Replace errors with fact
When you see misrepresentations made about the Air Force in social media, you may certainly identify and correct the error. Always do so with respect and with the facts. When you speak to someone who has an adversarial position, make sure what you say is factual and respectful. Don't argue, just correct the record.

7) Be aware of the image you present
Any time you engage in social media, you're representing the Air Force. Don't do anything that discredits you or our service.

8) Be cautious with information sharing
Maintain privacy settings on your social media accounts change your passwords regularly and don't give out personally identifiable information. Be cautious about the personal details you share on the Internet.

9) Avoid the offensive
Don't post any defamatory, libelous, vulgar, obscene, abusive, profane, threatening, racially or ethnically hateful or otherwise offensive or illegal information or material.

10) Don't violate privacy
Don't post any information that would infringe upon the proprietary, privacy or personal rights of others.

11) Don't violate copyright
Don't post any information or other material protected by copyright without the permission of the copyright owner.

12) Don't misuse trademarks

Don't use any words, logos or other marks that would infringe upon the trademark, service mark, certification mark or other intellectual property rights of the owners of such marks without owner permission.

13) No endorsements

Don't use the Air Force name to endorse or promote products, political positions or religious ideologies.

14) No impersonations

Don't manipulate identifiers in your post in an attempt to disguise, impersonate or otherwise misrepresent your identity or affiliation with any other person or entity.

15) Don't promote yourself for personal or financial gain

Don't use your Air Force affiliation, official title or position to promote, endorse or benefit yourself or any profit-making group or agency.

16) Follow terms of service

Become familiar with each social media site's terms of service and follow them. For example, having two personal profiles on Facebook violates their terms of service.

Home > AF Sites > Social Media Sites

SOCIAL MEDIA

Welcome to the Air Force social media directory! The directory is a one-stop shop of official Air Force social media pages across various social media sites.

Social media is all about collaboration, and we want to hear from you. Check out our pages, ask questions, provide feedback and share your thoughts.

Do you have an official U.S. Air Force social media page(s) you'd like included in this directory? If so, please submit the link, using an official e-mail account, and we'll get it added to the page.

DIRECTORY

SOCIAL MEDIA SITES

- Social Media Site : Facebook (510)
- Social Media Site : Twitter (202)
- Social Media Site : YouTube (121)
- Social Media Site : Flickr (54)
- Social Media Site : Instagram (9)
- Social Media Site : Blog (12)
- Social Media Site : LinkedIn (1)
- Social Media Site : (1)
- Social Media Site : Google+ (1)

SOCIAL MEDIA GUIDE

The U.S. Air Force social media directory

The external social media policy

The external social media policy is intended to provide all users a clear understanding of how the organization uses social media and how it promotes a fair engagement with its online community.

The core component of this document is the moderation policy, which should set ground rules for public participation in online engagement initiatives. The rules should have a positive spin and should be framed in such a way that they encourage participation and discourage anti-social, irrelevant, offensive, spam or inappropriate commercial submissions.

It's important to prepare a balanced policy. An overly restrictive moderation approach may create perceptions of censorship, while a policy that's too soft could result in receiving large volumes of inappropriate or non-constructive comments. This may have the effect of discouraging participation by other users. A well-crafted moderation policy will encourage participation and at the same time give the organization the justification it needs to remove or prevent inappropriate material from being published online.

In some cases it will be possible to review and approve all user-submitted content before it appears online. This approach minimizes the risk of inappropriate material, but it can be intensive in terms of staff time and it may also have a negative effect on user participation. It is advisable to choose a post-moderation approach, which allows all user-submitted content to appear online automatically. The content that doesn't respect the criteria set in the moderation policy (i.e., offensive or hateful language, obscene content, defamatory statements or unlawful material) will then be removed by the social media managers. In case of content removal, it could be beneficial to have pre-prepared messages addressing this kind of situation.

Social media policy for specific platforms

Usually the external social media policy embraces all the organization's channels. But sometimes it could be helpful to create a single policy for specific platforms, such as Facebook or Twitter.

The Twitter account of the Irish Embassy to the U.S.

For instance, this is the **Twitter Policy** of the Irish Foreign Affairs Ministry. Almost all the embassies' Twitter accounts have a link to the following document:

If you follow us, you can expect tweets covering some or all of the following:
Press Releases on the Departments activities and Ministerial speeches

Event information and occasional live coverage of events
Alerts about new content on our website
Emergency communications – for example changes to the Department's Travel Advice
Other practical information on services available through the Department

RTs ≠ Endorsement

Who we follow
If you follow us, we will not automatically follow you back. This is to help our followers identify other Twitter accounts that we are following such as other DFAT Twitter accounts, other Government Departments, Houses of the Oireachtas, relevant European institutions and accounts of particular relevance to Ireland.

@Replies and Direct Messages
We welcome feedback from our followers and will try to join the conversation where possible. However, we may not be able to reply individually to all the messages we receive via Twitter. The best means of communicating a query to us is by using the Submit Query link on our website or the relevant Embassy's website.

Please do not include personal/private information in your tweets to us.

Availability
Twitter may occasionally be unavailable and we accept no responsibility for lack of service due to Twitter downtime.

CHAPTER 6
TWITTER

Why use Twitter?

Twitter is an online social networking service that enables users to send and read short 140-character messages called "tweets". Users can access Twitter through the website interface or mobile device apps.

The 140-character limit is a challenge for diplomats. Many of them argue that it is too shallow to summarize complex issues such as those of international politics in a few short messages. It is evident that Twitter is not a tool for in-depth analysis. However, it can be very useful to inform quickly, to convey key messages, to monitor public opinion, to interact directly with users and to disseminate links to more thorough content.

If used well, it can effectively boost the communication strategy of an international organization by supporting activities such as media relations, PR outreach, events, etc.

Twitter is immediate and easy to use. It's a valuable source of information, and it allows one to build relationships with opinion-makers and to reach global audiences. Thanks to these key elements, it has become the preferred tool for governments' officials, diplomats and international officers worldwide.

According to the latest Burson-Marsteller's **Twiplomacy Report**, an annual study looking at the use of Twitter by governments worldwide, the vast majority (83%) of the 193 United Nations member countries has a presence on Twitter, more than two-thirds (68%) of all heads of state and heads of government has personal accounts and more than half of the world's foreign ministers and their institutions are active on the micro-blogging platforms launched in July 2006.

When Did They Start Tweeting?

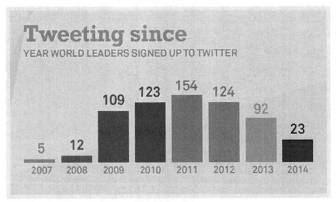

Source: 2014 Twiplomacy survey

Since the first message sent by co-founder Jack Dorsey, Twitter has grown exponentially, reaching 271 million monthly active users globally with more than 500 million tweets sent every day.

The quantitative statistics on the use of Twitter worldwide are relatively important in itself. It is more significant instead to note that Twitter is increasingly popular among the networks that diplomats or international officers have traditionally been called to cultivate: politicians, journalists, opinion-makers, government officials, businessmen, representatives of the cultural scene, etc. This makes Twitter a helpful tool to improve the public diplomacy activity.

The "Twiplomacy" birth

On December 2008, U.S. Deputy Assistant Secretary of State for Public Diplomacy Colleen Graffy gave a sudden, and maybe unintentional, push to the debate on digital diplomacy. During an official visit to some European countries she started tweeting personal views and funny stories regarding the private side of the trip. Her unusual tweets sparked a stimulating discussion among diplomats and journalists. Graffy's defenders emphasized that the confidential approach reflected Twitter's very nature and that it would have been incongruous to post messages in the bureaucratic style of the State Department. On the other side, Graffy's detractors pointed out that her tweets were just a shallow communication with no relevant content and that they could even be counterproductive for the U.S. reputation.

> **@Colleen_Graffy**
> Colleen Graffy
>
> Renting a bathing suit and getting ready to take the plunge into the geothermal hot springs and smear silica mud on my face
>
> 7 Dic 08 via mobile web

As she came back from the trip, Colleen Graffy sent an **op-ed** to *The Washington Post* to defend her choice of using Twitter in that way. It is worthwhile to report some excerpts:

"Not that long ago, communicating diplomat-to-diplomat was enough. Agreements were reached behind closed doors and announced in a manner and degree that suited the schedule and desires of the governments involved, not the general population. In fact, the public was by and large an afterthought. But the proliferation of democracies and the emergence of the round-the-clock media environment have brought an end to those days. Now, governments must communicate not only with their people but also with foreign audiences, including through public diplomacy

In short, public diplomacy is the art of communicating a country's policies, values and culture. If diplomats want to engage effectively with people, we first need to listen, then connect and then communicate. In the part of the world that I know and cover, Europe and Eurasia, most people are tuned in to television, and the younger generation is using text messages and the Internet. So, we need to be there, too...

Simply put, Twitter is just one more tool through which we can connect, and by linking my messages to video and photos, I can inform whole new audiences about U.S. views and ideas in a format with which they feel comfortable. Twitter blends the personal with the professional: To get your message across, you have to show there's a real person doing the posting....

The other reason to Twitter my trip was simple: Communicating in this peppy, informal medium helped to personalize my visit and enhance my impact as a U.S. official. When I met with students at the University of Bucharest, and later with Moldovan bloggers, we were connected before I even arrived. One young Romanian student said: "We feel like we already know you -- you are not some intimidating government official. We feel comfortable talking with you."
Isn't that what effective public diplomacy is about?

Six years have passed since that article, but I still consider Coleen Graffy's op-ed one of the best Twiplomacy manifestos.

Twitter basics

Let's start with a bunch of terms (and their abbreviations), which are essential for understanding how this social media works.

Tweet: a 140-character message (including spaces).

Retweet (RT): Re-sharing or giving credit to someone else's tweet.

Reply: When you want to reply to a particular tweet, you can click the Reply button. Replies appear in the recipient's feed as well as in the feed of those following both the sender and the recipient.

Mention (@): A way to reference another user by his username in a tweet. Users are notified when mentioned. It's a way to conduct discussions with other users in a public realm or notify them about content they might be interested in.

Useful Tip
Scrolling through your Twitter feed, you might see some tweet starting with a period before a username. That's because when you mention people in the beginning of your message, that tweet only comes up in the feeds of users who follow both you and the person you are directly tweeting at. So, if you want to tweet directly at someone and you want all of your followers to receive it in their feeds, add a period before you mention the person.

Direct Message (DM): A private, 140-character message between two people.

Hashtag (#): A way to denote a topic of conversation or participate in a larger linked discussion. A hashtag is a discovery tool that allows others to find your tweets, based on topics. Clicking on a hashtag, you can see all the tweets that mention it in real time — even from people you don't follow.

Feed: The stream of tweets you see on your homepage.

Setting your Twitter profile

When you open a profile on Twitter you must choose a username and name.

Username: it's a key element of your identity on Twitter. It appears in your profile URL and is unique to you. It will be displayed when people mention you, reply to your tweets or add you in a conversation.

Name: it is a personal identifier (most times the real name) displayed on your profile page and used to identify you, especially if your username is a nickname or describes the official position (ex: USAmbtoPoland).

Here are some tips to keep in mind when choosing a Twitter username:

- The username can contain up to 15 characters.
- The only characters you can use are uppercase and lowercase letters, numbers, and the underscore character.
- The best username is the same, or similar to, your own name. If another user has already claimed your name, try adding an underscore character or shortening your first name. Avoid adding shortened official titles (i.e., AmbWhite, DocStuart, HonAnderson).

When you see a blue badge next to a user's name on the profile page, it means Twitter has verified the authenticity of that profile.

Foreign ministries and ministers, diplomatic missions, ambassadors, international organizations and international high ranking officials are entitled to ask Twitter to verify their accounts. It is advisable to do it. The process can take time. Twitter deals with a high volume of verification requests and it focuses first on the most "highly sought users."

The official Twitter account of the Russian Foreign Ministry

Biography

Your profile bio must be 160 characters or fewer. It is recommendable to include both details about your official position as well as personal elements. It is possible to use a hashtag and to mention other profiles. Below the bio you can add your location and a website address.

Here are some examples from the community of foreign ambassadors to the US who use Twitter.

Mike Moore @NZAmbassadorUS
New Zealand Ambassador to the United States.
Comment: Formal and concise. Too concise. There is still place to add something more.

Björn Lyrvall @bjornly
Ambassador of Sweden to the United States. RT does not necessarily mean endorsement. Embassy of Sweden is @SwedeninUSA
Comment: Plain and formal, but at least includes the account of the mission and specifies that retweets are not an endorsement (see below about this feature). It also advertises the embassy's account. Good.

Gyorgy Szapary @AmbSzapary
Ambassador of Hungary to the United States. Economist, former Deputy Governor of the Hungarian Central Bank, former IMF official.
Comment: It's good to add some information about your professional background, but only if it is relevant.

Peter Taksøe-Jensen @petertaksoe
Ambassador of Denmark to the United States. I Tweet on Transatlantic Relations, Green Economy, the Arctic & more. RT's # endorsement.
Comment: Adding the main topics you address on Twitter is a good way to introduce yourself. The use of keywords also makes your account more searchable.

Muktar Djumaliev @MuktarDjumaliev
Ambassador of Kyrgyzstan 2 USA & Canada
Comment: Informality is ok, but it doesn't mean you have to write like a teenager.

It would be advisable to add some personal detail in your biography. Do you play soccer? Are you a wine enthusiast? Do you like cycling? Well, it's fine to add this information right after your official position. It makes you more human and helps fill the gap with your potential audience. Example:

Samatha Power *@AmbassadorPower*
United States Ambassador to the United Nations, mother, human rights defender, teacher, writer, and member of #RedSoxNation.

Adding personal information is good, but don't exaggerate, like Hillary Clinton:

Wife, mom, lawyer, women & kids advocate, FLOAR, FLOTUS, US Senator, SecState, author, dog owner, hair icon, pantsuit aficionado, glass ceiling cracker, TBD...

RT ≠ endorsement

Many users' profiles say: "Retweets are not endorsement". Sometimes social media policy of organizations and companies warn their employees about the dangers of retweeting messages of other users.

The Associated Press social media guidelines, for instance, states that:

Retweets, like tweets, should not be written in a way that looks like you're expressing a personal opinion on the issues of the day. A retweet with no comment of your own can easily be seen as a sign of approval of what you're relaying...However, we can judiciously retweet opinionated material if we make clear we're simply reporting it, much as we would quote it in a story. Colons and quote marks help make the distinction...

Actually, RT never meant endorsement. It is a way to pass on information or to say, "Did you hear that..." or, "I thought this was interesting". By retweeting you are not suggesting you should believe what others say, nor are you agreeing with or endorsing it. That said, I think that writing in your profile *RT # endorsement* will not save you if you retweet something inappropriate.

On October 2011 the Canadian government forced the chargé d'affaires of the Palestinian delegation to Ottawa to resign after she retweeted a message with a link to a YouTube video showing a Palestinian girl reciting a poem in Arabic. The English subtitles on the video included a passage where millions were called "to a war that raze the injustice and oppression and destroy the Jews." She apologized by saying she retweeted the link without watching the video.This episode should not prevent you from using the retweet button, which can be helpful to share interesting content, show other users the topics you are interested in, start a discussion, strengthen relations or show that you are not using Twitter just to convey your messages.

In addition to putting RT # endorsement in your profile, I strongly advise to carefully read or watch everything you are going to retweet and to be fully aware of who is the author of the content (tweet, article, video, photo) that you are sharing.

Tell who you are with good pictures
You must reinforce your profile with a good profile photo and a header picture. These photos are visible on all official Twitter platforms (desktop, mobile, third-party apps, etc.) when someone visits your profile.

Recommended dimensions for the **profile photo** are 400x400 pixels. Choose a picture of you smiling, with a plain background and don't include other people. You don't necessarily have to use a picture with a formal suit and tie, but at the same time, a photo of you on the beach wouldn't be advisable.

Recommended dimensions for the **header photo** are 1500x500 pixels. If you work in a diplomatic mission, it would be great to use a picture representing the bilateral ties between the two countries. You can even be (wisely) creative: for example you could use a picture of a beautiful place in your country with the name of the location and change it every month. Try to avoid boring pictures of you speaking at conferences or other formal events.

Don't underestimate the visual elements. They are very important, not only for your profile. According to Twitter, including photos in your messages boosts retweets by 62%.

Launch your account
Once your profile is ready, you should think about a good opening tweet. The CIA's opening tweet is a great example of a message with personality and sense of humor:

We can neither confirm nor deny that this is our first tweet.

↩ Reply ♺ Retweet ★ Favorite ••• More

RETWEETS   FAVORITES
72,980   36,743

7:49 PM - 6 Jun 2014

Before starting to follow people or to join conversations, it is strongly advisable to write some tweets, so you provide users with an immediate glance at the topics you will address and the general tone of your communication.

If you have followed the tips provided by this book, before launching your account you should already have monitored Twitter for a while and identified a list of people worth to follow. Once you have published the first couple of tweets, start to follow people, to favorite their tweets and to retweet or comment on the content they share.

What to tweet

Your goals and your target audience will determine what, when and how to tweet.

Always remember that Twitter is a social media and people expect at least a minimum level of interaction. Don't use Twitter as a microphone to spread your messages. In order to use this tool consistently, I suggest designing a specific Twitter content plan, where you can enlist topics, news and information you are going to tweet or retweet.

Here are some ideas for your content plan:

- Tweet about what you and your organization are doing. Share links to documents, programs, events, etc. Try to do it with a casual yet informative style.

- Transform the press release of your organization in a bunch of engaging tweets. Remember to share numbers (tweets with digits or numbers get 16% more retweets).

- If you work in a diplomatic mission, share important goals achieved by your governments, good performances of your country's economy, great business stories of companies, etc.

- Promote your country by periodically posting pictures or videos of gorgeous places or relevant cultural events.

- Tweet links to relevant articles from different sources. You can even add brief comments. Users will identify you as a person worth following independently from your official role.

- Share personal information (with moderation). Show your "human" side beyond the official role. It resonates well with followers. Authenticity helps building relationships and trust.

- I strongly advise avoiding jokes. The sense of humor varies greatly among cultures. The joke that makes you smile might be offensive in another country. Social media is about authenticity, not being funny.

- Show behind-the-scene actions. A picture of an informal chat between two political leaders is more powerful than the old style group photo. This can be a good opportunity to establish an informal relationship with your followers, but can also be risky, so be careful and think twice before pushing "send".

- Be open: reply to comments and criticisms. Welcome feedback and ideas. Participate in conversations and retweet other users' messages. Show that you fully understand that Twitter is not just a microphone.

The Turkish Foreign Ministry's official account

How to write good tweets

Keep the tweet short. It's not easy, but keeping your messages shorter than the allotted 140 characters will improve retweets, comments and conversations. Several studies saw a spike in retweets among those in the 70-100 character range.

Don't mix up topics and news. Each tweet should focus only on one thing; plan how to feed unrelated information in at different intervals instead.

Write well. You have very few words, so make them count. Find descriptive, powerful and appealing words.

Keep Tweets conversational. Be professional without being overly formal. Avoid business jargon when possible.

Use action words. A recent study by social media company Hubspot found that tweets containing more adverbs and verbs have a higher click-through rate than tweets with more nouns and adjectives. So the general rule that action words make for stronger, more compelling writing is also true for tweets.

Use hashtags. One or two hashtags can get you up to two times more engagement than tweets without hashtags, according to a study by Buddy Media/Salesforce. Choose the hashtags carefully, because if you use more than two your engagement will likely drop.

Add photos. According to a Twitter study that analyzed more than 2 million tweets, including photos in your messages boosts the engagement by 62%.

The power of visuals

The days when your Twitter feed was just a list of short messages are over. Now photos and video must play a key role in your editorial plan for this platform, as well as for other social media.

Over the last year Twitter has increased its visual pattern. Since October 2013, previews of photos and videos from Vine (the service that allows users to record and edit six-second long looping video clips) are displayed front and center in tweets. To see more of the photo or play the video, you just need to click the image. Twitter implemented this new feature by saying that "these rich tweets can bring your followers closer to what's happening and make them feel like they are right there with you." Now the Twitter feed looks a lot more like Facebook and is consistent with the big trend affecting social media: the predominant diffusion of the visual element.

Twitter has developed new features and tools to enhance the photos:

1) Sharing up to 4 photos in a single Tweet
It's possible to upload a series of photos that automatically create a collage. Just tap on a preview to get the full image and slide through the group. That allows, for instance, visually showcasing an event with only one tweet. Photos are displayed as a preview collage in your followers' timeline. They can then click on the collage to expand it and see each picture individually.

2) Photo tagging
It is possible to tag up to ten people in a single photo. Tagging doesn't affect character count in the tweet. Tagged users get a notification.

3) Filters
It is possible to make the photos look more expressive by adding eight filters, ranging from "vintage" to "black and white". Filters only work on mobile apps.

How to find people to follow
Figuring out who to follow and how to find them can be overwhelming at first. Twitter gives you several different ways to connect to relevant people you want to know.

1) The #Discover tab in the top navigation bar is the first place to find new people to follow. It showcases a list of tweets tailored on your interest. Moreover, in the left navigation pane you can find the following options:

Who to follow: Find suggestions based on the accounts you already follow (if you added any during the signup process).
Find contacts: Find people you know by searching your social or professional contacts on Gmail, Yahoo! or Outlook. Just select any service you use, and sign in when prompted to give Twitter access to your personal connections.
Popular accounts: Find accounts browsing categories of your interest.

2) Search for hashtags: in the search window on the right side of the top navigation bar, you can look for relevant #hashtags related to your interests or activity and you will see all the tweets containing that keyword as well as a list of users discussing that topic.

3) Analyze your favorite Twitter accounts: who do they follow, who also follows them and who do they talk to most? They might also have public lists of users divided per subject.
If someone adds you to a list, check out that list to see if there are interesting users to follow.

Building lists
If you are not familiar with Twitter, maybe you heard about lists on Twitter for the first time in the previous paragraph. The fact is that the ability to create lists in Twitter is a feature that's seriously underutilized. A list is a curated group of Twitter users. You can create your own lists or subscribe to lists created by others. Lists help you organize your Twitter feed so you can see only tweets coming from people on a specific list.

When you follow people on Twitter, their updates appear in real time on your stream timeline. As you begin to follow more and more people, you might benefit from lists that can help you manage the overwhelming flow of information.

For example, the State Department account @StateDept uses this feature to organize the flow of news of its various divisions: embassies, consulates, foreign-language accounts, etc.

You can create a list with journalists, another one with politicians or another one with users related to your strategic topics or users that advocate your organization.

As you explore Twitter and find interesting accounts, click the gear icon that appears on any user and select "Add or remove from lists". You might also search for a hashtag and add all the resulting users who pop up to make a list. One of the great things about lists is that you don't have to build all your lists yourself. You can subscribe to other people's lists. For example, you can subscribe to your favorite account's list of journalists or bloggers and Twitter will essentially bookmark that list for you.

Two important things to know about lists: 1) you don't have to be following a user in order to add him or her to a list; 2) tweets of users included in your lists but that you don't follow do not show up in your primary feed.

Interacting with users: how to organize a tweetchat

A tweetchat is a way to get people together at a predetermined time and talk about a subject. For a diplomatic mission, the purpose of organizing a tweetchat is to demonstrate an open approach by stirring conversations and connecting with people. Several Foreign Affairs ministers, ambassadors or high ranking officials of international organizations are increasingly using this tool to engage with foreign audiences as well as to gather information on people's views about specific topics.

Here are 5 steps to organize an effective tweetchat:

1) Choose the right #Hashtag - You have different options: you can choose a new hashtag for a specific tweetchat, or you can use the same hashtag every time you organize a conversation with online users. Start promoting the hashtag before the tweetchat.

2) Time and Duration - Select the time carefully and based on the local users' habits. For organizations, usually a good timetable might be early afternoon during a working day. Check in advance if there are important online or offline events already scheduled. The duration of a tweetchat can be a minimum of 30 minutes and a maximum of an hour.

3) Promotion - Promote your tweetchat on Twitter as well as on other social media platforms and on your website. Invite online influencers or ask them to help you share the event. You can even send a press note to journalists inviting them to follow it. Always remember that the aim of the tweetchat is to stimulate an open dialogue with people, so don't answer only questions coming from journalists or other influencers.

4) Prepare yourself - Organize talking points. Anticipate tough questions. Draft possible answers. Alert colleagues of various sections who can give support by providing pre-approved answers or useful documents. Prepare nice opening and closing tweets. Identify the staff that will help choose the relevant questions and write the replies during the tweetchat.

5) Aftermath. Collect all the tweets with online tools like Storify, which allows you to embed questions, answers and comments on your website. Choose some key messages emerged in the tweetchat and highlight them with a news post on your website or on other social media channels. Measure the participation and the total reach of the tweetchat. Analyze the most common questions and criticisms. Identify new active users to follow.

Former U.S. Ambassador to Russia Michael McFaul during a Tweetchat

Twitter advertising

The Twitter advertising system allows you to reach targeted audiences of users likely to be interested in your activity. To get started, log in with your usual username and password to the **Twitter Ads page**, where you can choose a campaign type:

Followers
This type of campaigns is the best way to grow your audience on Twitter.

Website click or conversions
Website click campaigns are optimized to drive traffic and generate conversions on your website from tweets targeted to specific audiences of users.

Tweet engagements

These campaigns are designed to reach more people and drive conversion for your organization.

Any tweet you publish organically on your Twitter account can be promoted to reach targeted audiences of users who do not follow your account.

App installs or engagements

With mobile app promotions, advertisers can drive users to download or open mobile apps directly from within a Tweet.

Leads on Twitter

Through this type of campaign people can seamlessly and securely share their email address without leaving Twitter or having to fill out a cumbersome form.

The last option allows you to create a custom campaign using the **old Promoted Tweets form**. One of the most popular uses of Twitter advertising is to promote a specific tweet. For example, if you search for a particular keyword, you're likely to see a promoted tweet at the top of the search results. You can choose to target users based on keywords that users search or tweet about, television programming they engage with and interests they cultivate. Interest-based targeting allows you to target people similar to the followers of any Twitter username you enter.

PM of Israel @IsraeliPM 8h
SHARE: Hamas's rejection of the cease fire gives Israel full legitimacy to expand the operation to protect our people

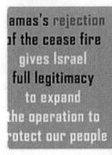

 Promoted by PM of Israel

↩   ↻ 1,150 ★ 529   +👤

A tweet promoted by the Israeli government

How much does advertising on Twitter cost? It depends. The cost per new follower, for instance, is set by a second price auction among other advertisers. Twitter states that "a bid of $2.50 - $3.50 is recommended based on historical averages." If you run a website clicks campaign, you will only be charged for the clicks to your website that are acquired from that campaign. All other actions and engagements (impressions, replies and retweets, for example) are free.

During the campaign setup process you will specify the maximum amount you are willing to pay for each action acquired through that campaign. This amount is your bid. As for Facebook, in order to avoid the waste of resources it is strongly advisable to ask the support of a social media marketing professional in case you decide to use the Twitter advertising system.

However, here are 4 tips you can bear in mind to effectively advertise on Twitter:

Use multimedia. To get the most out of your ads be sure that your content includes eye-catching imagery.

Offer compelling content. Promoted tweets, for instance, can be seen as invasive by users who still see their stream as a protected domain. So be sure to promote valuable content for your target audience.

Keep your profile updated and active. One of the likely effects of the ads campaign is that new people will discover your profile, so it is important to keep it up to date and full of relevant content and engaging visuals.

Use hashtags. When preparing the text of your ad campaign always include one or a maximum of two in the copy to your advantage.

CHAPTER 7
FACEBOOK

5 things to ponder before opening a Facebook Page

Since February 2004, when then 19-year-old Mark Zuckerberg founded it, Facebook has become the most popular social network worldwide, with impressive statistics:

Monthly active users: 1,4 billion
Daily active users: 829 million
Every 60 seconds on Facebook: 510 comments, 293,000 status updates and 136,000 photos.

A Facebook page is a great opportunity for businesses as well as for governments and public organizations to engage a wide audience, but managing it is challenging, more than what people usually think. Before joining Facebook it is advisable to take into consideration the following elements:

Resources: effectively managing a Facebook page takes time and resources, both human and financial, because it is useless to transfer press releases on Facebook without at least presenting them in a more appealing and engaging style. Creating and adapting content for social media is not free.

Plus, the content of a diplomatic mission should be disseminated mostly in the local language. In all the US embassies abroad there is at least one social media manager, often a local employee, whose job is to monitor the social platforms, post content and manage conversations. A small diplomatic mission might not afford an internal social media manager and could rely only on a "techie" employee who likely has not the adequate skills to professionally manage the page.

Advertising budget: the days of getting any free reach on Facebook are over. Since the end of 2013, the portion of Facebook fans who see content published by brands or organizations not supported by advertising has dramatically dropped. Nowadays, if you publish a post without boosting it with advertising, you can reasonably expect that less than 5% of your fans will see it in their newsfeed. Therefore, if you decide to open a Facebook page, you must consider allocating some advertising budget to promote your content.

A new and rapid approval process: stimulating and handling conversations or replying to comments and criticisms imply a deep review of the internal approval process. On social media it's not possible to wait days to get the official green light for a reply.

Audience: one of the biggest potentials of Facebook is the possibility to reach a large and heterogeneous community of users.

This platform can be valuable if one of the goals of the diplomatic mission is to expand the traditional niche audience. Otherwise, if this is not the goal and the target audience is narrow (journalists, international relations experts, academics, politicians, etc.) it might be advisable not to use Facebook, but rather other social media such as Twitter.

Mix of content: if you want to reach new audiences, then you must assess whether you are able to create and manage content that can attract this new range of users. You should be prepared to share "hard" content such as news about foreign, economic or human rights issues, as well as to produce "soft" content about music, sports, food or movies.

Setting up a Facebook page

If you have carefully considered the previous elements and you are still determined to open a Facebook page, these are the steps to follow.

Log in with a personal account and navigate to https://www.facebook.com/pages/create.php. This page will showcase six different classifications to choose from:
- Local Business or Place
- Company, Organization or Institution
- Brand or Product
- Artist, Band, or Public Figure
- Entertainment
- Cause or Community

Select the second option: company, organization or institution. You'll be asked to choose the category (government organization, NGO, etc.) and to insert the official name. I recommend carefully selecting your name. Although Facebook allows you to change your name, it's a tedious process and after 200 Likes you need Facebook's approval, which can take time.

Now Facebook will walk you through the following four basic sections to complete the fundamental aspects of your Page:

About
This section will showcase the main description for your organization. It can be up to 255 characters and appears on your main page. Introduce your organization and highlight why someone should 'like' your page.

Be sure to include a link to your website as well. The About section is also where you can select your unique domain (it can only be changed once).

Profile Picture
This will serve as the main visual icon of your page, appearing in search results and alongside any comments you publish. The recommended size is 180 x 180 pixels.

Add to Favorites
This step is totally optional, but can help you find your Page more easily. Every individual Facebook user has a vertical navigation bar to the left of their News Feed. You can add your Business Page as a "Favorite" item here for easy access.

Reach More People
Facebook will prompt you to create an advertisement to draw attention to your Page. Whether employing paid tactics is a part of your strategy or not, don't start any ads at this stage. So, skip this step.

Your page is now live. Facebook will ask if you'd like to "Like" it, but I recommend avoid doing it at the moment. This activity will appear in news feeds of your personal contacts on Facebook. Do it only after having published some compelling content that can convince people to like your page.

In the top navigation, you'll see an option for "Settings." If you click it, a vertical navigation bar with different sections should appear. We'll focus on three core ones:

Page Info
This is where you can add additional details about your organization.
Writing a good description with the right keywords will help your page's visibility both on Google and Facebook search engines.

Notifications
This section allows you to customize when and how you'd like to receive alerts about comments, messages, etc.

Page Roles
You can invite other colleagues to administer the Page or just to add content. There are five different types of roles for people who manage Pages. Only an admin can change someone's role. The table below outlines the five page roles and what they're able to do:

	Admin	Editor	Moderator	Advertiser	Analyst
Manage Page roles and settings	✓				
Edit the Page and add apps	✓	✓			
Create and delete posts as the Page	✓	✓			
Respond to and delete comments and posts to the Page	✓	✓	✓		
Send messages as the Page	✓	✓	✓		
Create ads	✓	✓	✓	✓	
View insights	✓	✓	✓	✓	✓
See who posted as the Page	✓	✓	✓	✓	✓

There is one last step before starting to publish: upload the cover photo. This is the large, horizontal image that spans the top of your Facebook Page. The official photo dimensions are 851x315 pixels. You can change it periodically to promote important events or highlight major initiatives of your organization.

The US Embassy to Italy uses the cover photo to highlight the initiative "Become a Student Ambassador" on its Facebook page.

Content strategy

Now that the page is ready, it's time to publish content. It's easy to get wrapped up in the technology when talking about social media, but the tools alone won't make your outreach activity effective. Good content does.

Your content should be:
• Relevant, useful and interesting
• Easy to understand and share
• Friendly, conversational and engaging
• Action-oriented

Because your target audience can receive multiple messages from multiple sources every day, try to create content that matches your audience's expectations, offer them valuable information or something that captures their attention. And try to do it using compelling language.

How to write on Facebook

Here are some basic principles to write a good Facebook post:

- Keep it short
- Include a link to longer content
- Write in a friendly (but professional) tone
- Write in active voice
- Limit use of jargon and technical language
- Don't use acronyms
- Ask the opinion of your followers
- Include calls to action
- Use numbers when they help you make your point
- Use hashtags to maximize the reach

Facebook offers more space to create content than Twitter: each post can be a maximum of 8.000 characters plus a link. However, a shorter length is recommended: posts of around 250 characters or shorter can be viewed completely in the newsfeed from a desktop. And statistics report that shorter posts are more likely to be shared: text with 80 characters or less get 66% more engagement (replies, share, comments).

This is what Facebook states about engagement:

Generally, the most engaging Page posts are short, original, benefit the person viewing the content and connect to your objectives and identity.

People tend to respond well to the following types of posts:

Photos and videos: Bright, colorful images depicting human interaction are particularly successful.

Questions: Asking questions encourages interaction and tells people their opinions matter. When you ask for feedback or thoughts, make sure to respond in the comments so people know you're listening.

The importance of visual content

Writing a good and brief text for your posts is essential, but you should consider that all the studies from any company that has analyzed Facebook data agrees on one point: pictures outperform everything. Images on Facebook Pages receive 53% more Likes, attract 104% more comments and get 83% more click-throughs than the average text posts (source: Hubspot Research).

Recommended size for shared pictures is 940x788 px.

A well-composed post with a nice picture published by the European Parliament

Geo-targeting features

Facebook provides some geo-localization features that make it possible to convey your messages to different foreign audiences. You can target each of your posts by language and/or geography (as specific as country, state, and city). Once you target your post, only the audiences you specified will see it in their newsfeed.

This feature can be helpful for the outreach strategy of international organizations and diplomatic missions. The Facebook page of an embassy, for instance, might have two different kinds of fans: its nationals and local citizens.

The kind of content, the language and even the style of the posts targeting these two publics are very different. The geo-targeting features allow you to send your audience content they value (and that they can read in their language!).

There are two possible options: geo-targeted posts and gated posts.

Geo-targeted posts

First, you have to enable geo-targeting in your settings. By default, this setting is turned off. Go to your Page Settings, click on "Edit Page" and choose "Edit Settings" from the drop-down menu. Under the "General" tab, go to "Post Targeting and Privacy" and turn the feature on.

To target one of your Facebook updates, select the targeting icon under your update. Then, click Add Targeting and select Location or Language from the drop-down menu to localize your post for a segment of your global audience.

If you chose Location, click the All Locations link that appears on the right side. Select Country, Region or State, or City. Type the name of the location, and select the correct location from the drop-down menu. You can add several locations by repeating this process. Then click Choose Locations.

If you chose to target by language, type in the name of the language, and select the correct language from the drop down menu. You can add several languages by repeating this process. You can target by both location and language (and you can even add other filters such as gender, age, interests, education, etc.). Facebook will tell you in real-time the estimated number of people you are targeting. This feature is very helpful because it gives you an idea if the intended audience is too big or too small.

Only the audience you specified will see your targeted post in their newsfeeds. Those outside your targeting criteria won't see the post, but they will be able to see it on your page. This isn't really something to be concerned about: fewer than 2% of people go back to the page after liking it. The vast majority of your fans will be consuming your content within their own newsfeed. But if you want to prevent people outside of your targeted criteria from seeing your post, even when they visit your page, you can use the second option: the gated posts.

Gated posts

First, click on the "Public" button next to the "Post" button. Add the locations of where you want to limit the visibility of your post or the language of your intended audience. Click post. Your content will now be viewable to the audience you targeted. The other users will not see your post, neither in their personal newsfeed nor on your page.

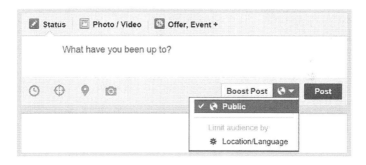

Facebook Advertising

Let's start with two definitions:

Organic reach: the total number of unique users who were shown your post through unpaid distribution.

Paid reach: the total number of unique users who were shown your post as a result of advertising. Several studies have recently highlighted a drastic decline of the organic reach of Facebook Pages. Gone are the days when Facebook used to show users mostly all the content posted by brands or organizations they liked. The current algorithms limit the reach of Pages' posts to less than 5% of people who follow them. Some marketers expect that it wouldn't be long before organic reach hit zero.

This trend has two implications: 1) opening a Facebook page without allocating some budget to promote your content can be ineffective; 2) to manage a Facebook Page you need skilled professionals who know how to use the advertising or at least a specific training program for those employees who are tasked to administer the Page.

How to master the Facebook advertising is worth a special guide and cannot be fully addressed in this book. What is important to highlight here is that it's still possible to improve the organic reach of your posts without spending a lot of money. Facebook's algorithm is constantly measuring the relative engagement between your brand and each individual user. If users visit your page, click your posts, like them, share them or comment on them, the so-called "engagement ranking" of the page increases. The higher this engagement, more likely it is that your posts will appear on your fans' newsfeeds.

Therefore, the challenge is to focus, more than ever before, on providing content that's interesting and relevant to the people you're trying to build relationships with.

Managing the conversations

Facebook is an open space where people tend to express their opinions straightforward.

Feedback and criticisms can give your organization an opportunity to deflect negativity and even improve your reputation, if you handle it right.

Before executing your social media strategy, you need to plan for the potential criticism that may come your way. There's no perfect way to respond and the answer usually depends on the type of criticism, how widespread it is, and where it is coming from. But it is possible to highlight some helpful guidelines:

Respond early and often. There's no greater insult to people commenting or criticizing your content or asking questions than to be ignored. Ignoring criticism might result in greater anger. Even if you don't have an immediate answer, tell the commentator that you hear them, acknowledge their complaint, and promise to investigate further.

Identify and ignore trolls. Some posters may be negative just to get attention, or their comments are just so over the top and rude that responding to them will only draw attention to an issue that that no one else is aware of. Sometimes it's just good to ignore these posts.

Delete comments only if they are particularly rude and they don't comply with your social media policy (see Chapter 4), where you should state that comments which defame, abuse, violate the legal rights of others or contain inappropriate language or obscene and indecent content will be removed.

Respond honestly and clearly. Just as you have to be authentic with your social media approach, you need to with your response, too. Admit mistakes when the fault is yours, and be inclusive in your responses.

Take the conversation offline. Sometimes it's better to ask the complainant to contact you directly via email. The goal here is putting the fire out by taking it offline and offering an open invite to continue the dialogue further and address the complainants' specific concerns.

Be prepared to change based on the feedback. If there's valid criticism about your outreach activity you should incorporate the feedback and make the appropriate changes. You'll win back trust quickly.

If possible, don't hesitate to bring humor to the situation. Practice shows some of the best responses on social media have been those that included a touch of self-effacing humor.

Use the same channels for the response. This may seem obvious, but it really isn't. Respond to people in the way they've criticized you. Don't send a press release to respond to a YouTube outburst.

The Facebook page of the U.S. Embassy to Pakistan

How to promote your page

After publishing the first set of compelling content, you can start promoting your page. The advantage of advertising your Facebook page is that when visitors click 'Like' and become fans, you establish a relationship with them and you can then "nurture" your community with valuable information and key messages. By promoting only your website, users might visit it and never return.

Here are some tips to promote your new Facebook page:

- **Invite users to Like the Page**. I recommend the following cadence: your colleagues, your close network of professional contacts, your network of journalists by telling them that you will also use the page to spread news, your whole network of contacts.

- **Show off your Page by adding a Facebook Like Box to your website**. It gives a nice impression of what to expect from your page by providing a preview of your latest posts.

- **Write an article on your website about the new Facebook Page** and give users compelling reasons to follow it.

- **If you've got an email list, send a quick email letting your subscribers know of your Facebook Page**. From now on, all future newsletters should have a link to your Facebook page as well.

- **Put the address of the Page in your email signature**.

- Promote your Facebook Page (and all your other social platforms) on your **business cards, flyers, brochures and other kinds of materials**.

- **Cross-promote your Page on other social channels**: for instance, include your fan page URL on your Twitter profile description or throw in a well-timed fan page link at the end of your YouTube videos.

- **Put your Page URL in all the official presentations/slides**.

- **Plan some budget to advertise your page on Facebook**, targeting specific audiences that will be interested in your activity.

Measuring your performances

In all social media strategies, content is key. Analyzing data of your Page and finding what content gets the best response allows you to attract new users and engage your fans. Social data is hugely powerful for driving your content strategy, as it can help you make a wide range of decisions, from which content to create to the weight of that content within your overall plan.

Facebook has embedded some helpful metrics: number of Likes, post reach, engagement rates and others, all of which will help you understand how your content is being received.

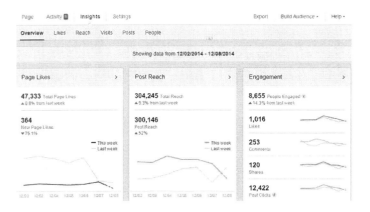

Click the "Insights" option in the top navigation of your Page and you will see the following:

Overview: This tab shows a 7-day snapshot of your metrics, such as Page Likes, post reach, and overall engagement.

Likes: This tab shows your overall fan growth and losses. If you're employing paid efforts, you'll be able to see the breakdown of paid versus organic growth.

Reach: this tab is probably one of the most useful: it allows you to see how many views each individual post received, therefore allowing you to formulate a good idea as to which content works best. From this data you can produce content in a similar format, to ensure you receive the highest engagement.

Visits: this tab informs you about where the traffic to your Facebook page came from. It's useful if you are trying to gear traffic from a particular source.

Posts: this tab is one of the more effective components to Facebook insights. It allows you to see exactly how many followers viewed your content at exactly what time. This is the perfect way to work out how and when to schedule your posts to receive the greatest amount of hits. The clock icon under the status update box allows you to schedule your posts, which means that they will go live at a time and date specified by you. This is particularly handy, especially if statistics say that your audience is active in the evening or during the week-end. If you decide to schedule content outside business hours, it's advisable to keep an eye on possible comments.

People: this tab gives you a geographical breakdown of the Page's fans, as well as showing the percentage of men and women.

How to track your "competitors"

Facebook Insights allows you to watch other Facebook pages so you can compare their activity, engagement and audience growth to your own.

The "**Pages to Watch**" feature is particularly handy if you want to see what's working for your competitors or similar niche pages. You can see exactly what content they're posting, how often they're posting, when they're posting and the resulting engagement. Armed with that information, you can tailor your own updates accordingly. To find the "Pages to Watch" feature, go click on Overview and scroll down the page to the Add Pages section (it's just below the Your 5 Most Recent Posts box).

To help you along, watch how often other pages post and how it affects their engagement. What time of day are they posting? What time of day results in the most comments, likes and shares? You have to experiment with your own page and post at those times as well to see if it affects your own page's engagement. Don't forget that each page is different and what works for similar organizations might not necessarily work for you.

CHAPTER 8
YOUTUBE

Why use YouTube?
Video marketing is fast becoming a popular way not only to showcase a product or to sell a service, but also to describe policies, to foster political campaigns or to explain a government's stance on a major international issue. Why? Because people love watching videos. With 3 billion searches a month, YouTube is currently the second-largest search engine after Google (who acquired YouTube in 2006).

Quick YouTube stats:
One billion unique users a month
Six billion hours of video watched each month
100 hours of video uploaded every minute

YouTube can be included in the communications strategy of an international organization for four main reasons:

1) It allows you to convey messages across a global platform that people increasingly use not only for fun but to get news and information about a wide range of topics.

2) Good quality videos can support your communications tactics: instead of sending out only a press release, it is possible to produce and share a video that media online and TVs can pick up.

3) YouTube offers the possibility to live stream events, thus amplifying the reach of your organization's programs.

4) YouTube is an excellent sharing platform. Once a video is uploaded on YouTube, it can be easily embedded on websites and blogs and can be shared across several social media channels such as Facebook, Twitter or LinkedIn.

I recognize that the association between diplomacy and videos is hard to accept, but there are several ways to creatively use the potential of videos to convey your messages.

Some videos a diplomatic mission might create:
- Welcome message of the ambassador
- Ambassador's statements on key topics
- Short interviews with other diplomats of the mission about various issues
- Videos to describe major initiatives of the mission
- How-to videos (i.e.: how to apply for a visa)
- Video excerpts of conferences and events
- Videos to promote the country (touristic locations, business opportunities, etc.)
- User-generated videos (i.e., by asking users to submit short videos of their vacations in your country)
- Videos with diplomats casually describing traditions, language, food or cultural habits of their country.

In recent years it has become standard practice for new U.S. ambassadors to make videos to introduce themselves to the local population before their departure. Someone argues that it can be considered a breach of the diplomatic rule that prevents the ambassadors from functioning in an official capacity until they have officially presented their credentials.

Beyond this criticism, this practice is interesting from a communication perspective and it is worth examining how the U.S. diplomats are using these videos to engage a broader audience by mixing both their professional and personal sides. Moreover, from a technical point of view the clips are well-filmed and edited, and you can take them as an inspiring model.

It is possible to watch all these videos on the YouTube **channel** of the US International Information Program.

Introducing Caroline Kennedy, U.S. Ambassador to Japan

Setting up a YouTube channel

Log in to YouTube with a Google account and click on your image thumbnail in the top right corner. Click on the gear icon next to the button that reads "Creator Studio." Click "create a new channel" and you'll see a page that looks like this.

You need to choose a name and the category that fits best. After this initial step you can customize your channel. The first two tabs to fill out with information are the "Home" and "About" tabs.

Home Tab

Your profile photo will default to the one of the Google+ account you used to create the channel. YouTube also has a big cover photo in its layout. To upload your photo, click the "Add channel art" button in the middle of the cover photo area. Alternatively, mouse-over the photo space to reveal an edit button in the upper right corner to open a drop-down menu. Select "Edit channel art" and then either drag or upload the image you want. The recommended file size is 2560 x 1440 pixels.

About Tab

After getting the visuals in place, click the "About" tab on your channel's home page. Three buttons will appear in this section to guide the further development of your YouTube account.

Channel description: In this text box, enter a description of your organization and the type of content that you plan to share.

Links: This section helps you connect YouTube to your other online profiles. You can select whether to display links overlaid on the cover photo and how many links will appear there. It also lets you decide whether or not to show how many views your channel has, and when you created the account.

Add Channels: Use this area to highlight YouTube channels of other organizations associated with you (in case of a diplomatic mission, you could link to the consulates' channels or to your government official channel). This section is optional; you can even leave it blank.

Good YouTube setup: US Embassy to Israel

Recommended format of your videos

After customizing your channel, you can start uploading videos and managing your page. One of the best YouTube features is the ability to support different video formats for uploading, thus making it easier for users to share their videos. In most cases, YouTube automatically optimizes your video, but some settings will give the best uploading results.

YouTube accepts resolutions up to 4K and file sizes of 2 GB. It also accepts almost all popular formats, but the best format to use is MP4. It's not as heavy as AVI and provides better quality than FLV.

It's recommended to upload videos in HD for quality playback. YouTube uses 16:9 aspect ratio players. If you are uploading a non-16:9 file, it will be processed and displayed correctly as well, with pillar boxes (black bars on the left and right) or letter boxes (black bars at the top and bottom) provided by the player. If you want to fit the player perfectly, encode at these resolutions:

2160p: 3840x2160
1440p: 2560x1440
1080p: 1920x1080
720p: 1280x720
480p: 854x480
360p: 640x360
240p: 426x240

Creating good videos

Every second, one hour of video is uploaded to YouTube. Due to this overwhelming amount of content ranging from music to sports, from funny videos to free training courses, users' attention on YouTube might be sporadic. Therefore it's important to catch the interest of your target audience with valuable content presented in a professional manner.

Though an increasing number of governments, diplomatic missions and international organizations is using YouTube, video isn't necessarily the right medium for everyone. Like any other kind of social media, it requires resources to create and promote the content and monitor the channel. A good video production is surely more expensive than a tweet. On the other hand, the availability of compact cameras able to film high definition videos and of easy-to-use video editing tools might help you to create good short videos that can be part of your content strategy.

It's fundamental to keep in mind that the optimum length of a video is around 90 seconds, which is ample time for you to get your message across. The first five seconds of any video is the most important part. You really need to grab the viewers' attention in this amount of time if you want them to watch the rest of your video. Unless you are interviewing a special person, videos of 30+ minutes are long gone, so bear this in mind when you produce your video. For a long video interview, you can plan to produce two different versions: a short one of about 2-3 minutes and a longer one.

YouTube is a global platform and offers diplomatic missions and international organizations helpful features to reach broad audiences, such as the possibility to add subtitles to the videos:

1) Visit your Video Manager and click the drop-down menu next to the "Edit" button for the video you'd like to add subtitles.
2) Select Subtitles and CC
3) Select the original language of the video from the drop-down menu (160 languages)
4) Click the Add subtitles or CC button
5) Choose the language of the subtitles or CC you would like to create and then choose one of the following options: "Create new subtitles or CC", "Transcribe and set timings", or "Upload a file".

The first option is user-friendly, especially if you are editing a short video. This is what you have to do:

-Play the video. When you get to the part where you want to add a subtitle, click pause.
- Type your subtitle into the box that says, "Type subtitles here," and click the blue button to create it. You'll see it show up in the transcript, and on the timeline below the video.
- Adjust when the subtitle starts and ends by dragging its handles.
- Repeat the process for all spoken words in the video.

Another useful feature allows you to add annotations, clickable text overlays on videos, to give more information, aid in navigation and boost engagement. Common uses of annotations include asking viewers to like, favorite or share a video, linking to related videos or content you reference in the video, linking to full versions of shorter video clips, creating a table of contents for long-form videos, and highlighting your website or your social media presence.

Filming an event

Here are some tips for filming conferences or events:

- Scout out your location before the day of the event to carefully plan shooting placements.

- Plan to film short interviews with the main speakers before or after the event so you can upload them on YouTube as well as the video of the whole event.

- Use two cameras, one with a wide shot of the stage and one with a close-up that follows the action.

- Make sure the lighting on stage is good for filming. Most of the non-professional cameras do a poor job under bad lighting, producing grainy and washed-out videos that can't be improved in post-production.

- Don't use shotgun microphones to record the audio; always get a direct line in. The microphones built into most camcorders are fairly basic.

 - If the presentation contains videos or slides, make sure to get a copy of those files. Filming the screen won't look very good.

- Shoot "B-roll", secondary footage that you splice into your primary video to flesh out the story.

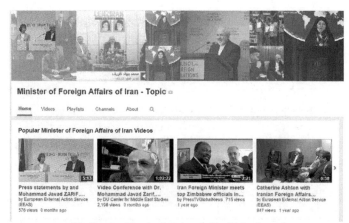

The Iranian Foreign Ministry's YouTube channel

How to Make Your Videos Rank Better on YouTube

Once you have uploaded your video, the next task is to make it rank high in the search results related to the topics of the video. It is essential to know the main criteria YouTube uses to rank content:

Relevant Keywords: Just as a webpage with relevant keyword terms and phrases always ranks better in search results, videos with the relevant keywords will appear at the top of YouTube search results.

Video Tags: Including a few keywords in the tag helps YouTube to know what your video is about.

Title: The video title is also an important factor in determining your YouTube video ranking.

Description: Description is important because that's what YouTube depends on to determine what your video is all about.

Video Transcript: YouTube uses the transcription to rank your video. To help YouTube get a summary of your video you can include the targeted keywords in the transcription.

Channel Authority: It can be established with more views and engagement of your audience.

Views and Video Retention: Number of views and how much time users spent watching your videos are key factors.

Comments: More comments on your video also give an authority signal to YouTube for your video.

Subscribes: If people have subscribed to your channel after watching your video, this means they have loved it. This indicates to YouTube as well as to Google that your video is authoritative.

Shares/Favorites/Thumbs up or down: Actions people make after watching your video can determine the ranking in the search results.

Tips to Rank Your Video Higher on YouTube

- Optimize Your Video Title and Description With Relevant Keywords: Make sure your video title and description contain the relevant keyword terms and phrases. Write around a 250-word description with the keywords included. Make sure the keywords are naturally incorporated and don't appear as spam.

- Optimize Video Tags: It is ideal to have six to eight relevant tags for your video.

- **Share** your video across various social media, embed it on your websites and blogs or post the link in your newsletter.

- **Use YouTube Analytics** to check your video's retention rate and track how long viewers watched your video and at exactly which point they stopped watching. You can then review your videos based on these inputs.

YouTube Analytics basics

With YouTube Analytics you can see tons of data, including who your viewers are, how much they are watching, and how engaging your videos are to them.

Knowing certain statistics and trends about your audience and how they watch your channel can inform the choices you make. YouTube Analytics provides actionable insights to make better videos, implement and measure optimizations and develop strategic programming.

Access YouTube Analytics directly through youtube.com/analytics. Then, use the left hand menu to navigate to all the different reports. At the top of many reports you can get the precise information you're looking for by filtering your reports by Content, Geography and Date.

You can see the number of views, the estimated minutes watched, the demographics of your audience, the level of engagement (likes, shares, etc) and the traffic sources.

The Traffic Sources report is helpful to assess your channel's performance. Understanding how people found your videos is particularly important for two reasons: 1) you can see if title, description, tags and keywords are doing well in ranking your video; 2) if you have an integrated social media strategy and you are sharing your videos on other platforms, you can monitor how many people discovered your videos through Twitter, Facebook, etc.

Are my videos engaging?
Understanding how audiences interact with your content can help you to create more engaging content. The key metrics are: 1) Absolute Retention: shows which parts of your video people are watching and/or abandoning; 2) Relative Retention: shows audience engagement compared to other videos of similar length. For example, significant dips in Absolute Retention within the first 5-10 seconds can indicate unmet audience expectations.

Other important insights of YouTube Analytics are included in the "Engagement report", which allows you to study the way users interact with your videos. Understanding which videos your audience interacts with most can help you craft more successful content and promotional strategies. Examine Likes, Dislikes, Comments, and Sharing on standout videos to understand what type of content resonates best with your target audience.

CHAPTER 9
GOOGLE+ and LINKEDIN

Why use Google+?
Google launched the Google+ service as an invitation-only "field test" on June 2011, but soon suspended early invites due to a huge demand for new accounts. The unexpected success made many marketers predict that Google+ would have rapidly overwhelmed Facebook. But it was a wrong forecast. Recent studies show that there are currently about 300 million active monthly users worldwide, thus making Google+ the second most popular social network in terms of geographic distribution, after Facebook. While official information isn't available, reports commonly estimate that the large majority of users are students, marketers, photographers and people working in the tech sector (developers, engineers, designers). Therefore, three years after its debut, Google+'s audience is still limited to narrow segments.

Thanks to its core feature, the "Circles", which enables users to organize people into groups, Google+ is far more easily customizable and allows a greater level of flexibility than Facebook or Twitter. For example, users can share content specific to their professional network with people in that circle, while sharing pictures of their vacation to a more private circle, all from the same platform.

Another feature that seems to be growing in popularity with users, brands and organizations is the Google+ Hangout. Hangouts can be public or invite-only and allow users to connect with voice and video without needing to download any software. Google has also added Communities, which appear to mirror Facebook's groups, giving additional functionality and interaction opportunity to the platform.

Despite these interesting features, Google+'s future is unpredictable. The departure in April 2014 of one of the co-founders spawned press speculation that Google would retire its social platform soon. The company refuted the speculation and pledged to continue development of Google+.

While it is extremely important to determine whether your target audience uses this platform, there are at least two main reasons to include Google+ in your social media strategy.

1) **High engagement level**: according to a recent Forrester study, G+ posts generate as much engagement (likes, comments, shares) as Facebook and twice as much as Twitter. Not everyone likes G+, but those that do, use it intensively.

2) **Better exposure in Google search results**: Google+ has incredible value in terms of SEO (Search Engine Optimization), as the most popular search engine indexes its own social platform better than any other social media, including Facebook, Twitter or LinkedIn.

The Google+ page of the U.S. Embassy in Manila

How to set up a Google+ page

To create a Google+ page, you must first have a personal profile. In the left-hand menu of your profile you can click "Pages" and then "Get your page" button. The second step involves choosing a category that defines your activity. The options are limited to "Storefront", "Service Area" or "Brand". You can select "Brand" and then choose a name and add your website. You may also choose to restrict who views your posts (these settings limit access for your content to certain ages or countries).

You now have an official page and the final step includes describing your activity, entering contact information, including external links to other social media platforms and choosing a branded profile photo (recommended size: at least 1000x1000 pixels).

Put an extra effort to make your page visually appealing by adding a captivating cover photo (recommended size: at least 2120x1192 pixels).

There are three types of admins for Google+ pages: owners, managers, and communications managers. Each page can only have one owner, but it can have up to 50 managers or communications managers. Adding managers allows you to share control of your page posting and settings with multiple people without having to share your personal login information. The following tab shows the capabilities of the different roles:

Capabilities	Owner	Manager	Communications Manager
Add/remove managers	✓		
Delete account	✓		
Edit profile	✓	✓	
Manage YouTube videos and Hangouts on Air	✓	✓	
Post to customers, respond to reviews, and view Insights	✓	✓	✓
Most other actions	✓	✓	✓

Google+ Circles

One of the prominent features of Google+ is the concept of "Circles." The platform allows you to classify your connections into different groups. By managing these circles effectively, you can share the right content with the right people. A diplomatic mission, for instance, might create one circle with local citizens and another one with its own nationals living in the host country. If it wants to promote a detailed guide on how to get a visa, it can share the post only with the local citizens.

Or, by creating a circle with media representatives, the embassy might send them press releases and in-depth information not worth sharing with the general public. It is also possible to create circles based on topics or specific interests (economy, cultural affairs, tourism, etc.). You can have the same person in several of your Circles. When you add someone to a Circle, they do get a notification, but it only tells them that you added them on Google+. They cannot see what groups you added them to.

Circles are also helpful to manage the information flow in your feed. You can decide to receive updates from all your connections or just from those in a specific Circle. You can even choose a different setting for each of your Circles by clicking the gear icon in the top right corner and selecting the amount of updates you want to receive from that list of users.

5 tips to share good content on Google+

1) Use Google+ as a microblogging platform. Even though Google+ has no character limit such as Twitter, it is important to keep your text as short as possible. Use links (to your website or other platforms) to direct users to more detailed information.

2) Don't just copy and paste official documents. Try to optimize your content by including hashtags, photos, infographics or videos. Maintain the frequency of your posts for the best results.

3) Optimize the first 45-50 characters of your posts because they will appear in Google's search results. Make sure to include any keywords you're trying to rank for.

4) Use visuals as frequently as possible. Like on Facebook, photos and videos can help boost your content even on Google+

5) Differentiate your content and target your posts using Circles. For example, you can share a detailed press release with your Circle of journalists and just a brief summary of the news supported by a compelling picture with the general public.

Google+ Hangout

On May 10, 2013 John Kerry became the first U.S. Secretary of State to take part in a Google+ Hangout, receiving questions about the U.S. foreign policy from several users. It was another important step in the digital diplomacy development.

John Kerry during his first Google+ Hangout

Hangouts are one of the most valuable Google+ features and allow you to go live for free on Google+, YouTube and your website. The video will be automatically recorded and saved on your YouTube channel. You can host interactive conversations with people by taking questions in advance from the community and answering them during the Hangout or by getting questions live through Google+ or other social media platforms.

How to set up a hangout:
Choose Hangouts in the Home menu of the Google+. Click Hangouts On Air and you will see a pop-up box where you can set the basics of your event. It's very important to choose a good title and a compelling description using relevant keywords related to the subject you are going to address. Every Hangout On Air is given a generic visual header, but it is advisable to personalize it in order to better promote the event (recommended size is 1200 x 300 pixels).

To make your Hangout On Air even more appealing, you can include a trailer. When someone visits your Hangout On Air page, instead of seeing only a countdown to your event, they will see a trailer video anticipating the topics and the speakers attending the event.

Now that your Hangout is set, what you have to do is spread the word on Google+, on your website and across all the other social media platforms. Hosting a Google Hangout On Air is an easy way to improve the reputation of your organization, show your willingness to build an interactive dialogue with the public and foster a sense of community.

Google+ Insights

On June 2014 Google launched new Insights reports featuring rich analytics that can help you measure your outreach efforts and optimize your content.

Currently the Insights page has three sections:

1) **Visibility**: you can see the number of cumulative views of the page and its content. You can see these views broken down into search, photo, post and profile views.

2) **Engagement**: you can see the total number of actions (+1, shares and comments) your content has received in the last 7, 30 or 90 days. For any of your posts, you can take a closer look at how each of them performed.

3) **Audience**: you can track the number of followers by country, gender and age.

It is also worth mentioning Google+ Ripples, a special analytic feature providing valuable insights around distribution channels, top influencers and share velocity for any given post. Organizations can use ripples to better understand who's shared their content and what effect those shares had on the post's overall visibility.

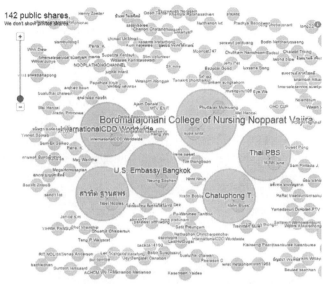

Ripples of a post published on Google+ by the U.S Embassy to Thailand. The big circles represent key online influencers who shared the post.

Ripples come out in a graphical presentation showing the following information:

1) Who has publicly shared a post and the comments they've made: people who have shared your link will be displayed with their own circle. Inside the circle will be people who have reshared the link from that person (and so on). Circles are roughly sized based on the relative influence of that person. For this reason Ripples is extremely helpful to identify top influencers among the target audience. The comments users added when they shared a link are also displayed in the sidebar of Ripples.

2) How a post or URL was shared over time

At the bottom of the Ripples page, you can play an animated version of the visualization that shows how the link was shared over time. You can also see a line graph that illustrates activity on the post.

3) Statistics on how a post or URL was shared

You can check out people who were sharing hubs (people who had the most reshares of the post), statistics for how the link was shared, and the native language breakdown in which the link was shared.

Ripples only uses public data, so there may be a discrepancy between the number of shares that you see on a post in the stream and the number of shares that Ripples displays. To view Ripples for a public post (not only yours, but also posts published by other users or organizations) just click the dropdown arrow at the top of the post you're curious about and click View Ripples.

Why use LinkedIn?

LinkedIn is the most popular business-oriented social networking service. It was launched on May 2003 and currently has more than 260 million users worldwide.

While the number of users is increasing, the key question is how many of those users actively access the site, keep their professional information up to date, share links, participate in discussions and generally engage with their peers? The reality is that after creating an account, most users add some connections and then sporadically access the site. One of the recognized limits of LinkedIn is, in fact, the low level of users' engagement.

Nevertheless, the platform has interesting features for international organizations, such as the possibility to target updates by geography or language, to create groups about specific topics, to promote economic initiatives among key influencers or to reach out a broad network of professional contacts.

How to create a LinkedIn Page

To create a page on LinkedIn you must own a personal profile and meet all of the following requirements:

You must have a personal LinkedIn profile set up with your true first and last name.
You must have several connections on your profile.
You're a current employee of the organization and your position is listed in the Experience section on your profile.

You have an official email address (e.g. john@companyname.com) added and confirmed on your LinkedIn account (domains like gmail.com or yahoo.com cannot be used to create a Company Page). Your organization's email domain is unique.

To start, move your cursor over "Interests" at the top of your homepage and select Companies. Click Create in the "Create a Company Page" box on the right. Enter your organization's official name and your work email address. Click Continue and enter information about your organization. You must include a description (250-2000 characters including spaces) and your official website address. Be aware that a preview of your page is not available. The page goes live as soon as you create it. You can choose multiple admins to manage the page, but you must be connected to these members on LinkedIn first.

It is advisable to improve the page by adding a compelling cover image and an official logo. Here are the file requirements:

Cover Image: Minimum 646x220 pixels, PNG/JPEG/GIF format, maximum 2 MB, landscape layout

Standard Logo: 100x60 pixels, PNG/JPEG/GIF format, maximum 2 MB, landscape layout

Square Logo (used on the network updates): 50x50 pixels, PNG/JPEG/GIF format, maximum 2 MB.

5 tips to attract followers to your page:

Engage the employees of your organization. Encourage them to create and complete LinkedIn profiles. Once they include the organization name, they automatically become followers of the page. Ask them to share your content and include a link to the page in their email signatures.

Promote the page outside the company. Link to the page in all your communications, like emails, newsletters or blog posts. Invite professional contacts, partners, and other key audiences to become followers.

Add a "Follow" button to your website. Convert visitors who come to your site by making it easy for them to simply click on a button to follow your page.

Launch an Ad campaign. Advertisings appear throughout LinkedIn and can be targeted to members in specific industries or regions to help you attract the right followers for your page. These ads encourage potential followers to click on the "Follow" button and join your page. When members follow your organization, that action spreads through their network as an update, which motivates others to follow too.

Take part in LinkedIn Groups. Join groups related to your activity to share valuable information and interact with key influencers.

The LinkedIn page of the U.S. embassy to Argentina

Linkedin geo-targeting features

LinkedIn offers several geo-targeting features to reach users worldwide. Here are some options:

Localized company names and descriptions - You can display your page's name and description in over 20 languages. Members will be able to see what your page shows for their language. If you haven't added language-specific information, they'll see the default name and description.

Additional admins - You can add other admins from regional offices and have them send updates targeted to their region.

Affiliated Pages - If you prefer not to provide regional teams access to the parent Page or if your regional teams need a fully distinct page presence, they can create an affiliated local Page.

Targeted updates - Updates can be targeted to the geographic locations and languages their audiences are in.

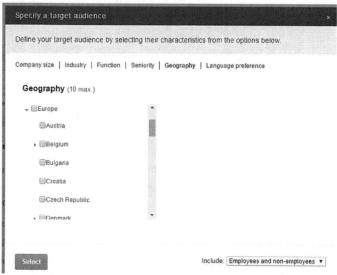

The box featuring all the targeting options for the updates

LinkedIn groups

One beneficial tactic is to be active with your personal profile in LinkedIn groups in order to expand your network of contacts.

To find relevant groups, go to the search bar at the top of your LinkedIn page, typing in an industry name or topic, and then selecting "Groups" from the dropdown menu on the left side of the search bar. LinkedIn will show you all the relevant groups in a search result page, generally sorted by the ones with the most members to the ones with the least.

Sort through groups using the numerous filters on the left side of the screen. For instance, you can see "Open groups" or "Closed groups," and search according to which groups include some of your connections. Keep in mind that closed groups require approval before you'll be admitted into the community.

Once you've been accepted into a group, you'll have options to change your notification settings. If you don't want to receive emails about all the updates within each of the groups you're a member of, turn off email notifications within the settings.

Now you can start commenting, sharing information or posing questions. You can even just monitor the ongoing discussions in order to find helpful information, see what types of topics generate the most attention or scout interesting contacts to reach out.

Instead of joining existing groups, an alternative way to make new connections might be to create your own group, for instance to promote an economic initiative or to address a specific community. Managing a group needs some effort, so it's better to carefully consider the following elements before opening a group:

What is the aim of the group?
What is the target audience?
Are there other similar groups?
Who is going to manage it?
What type of content can generate most interest?
What are the guidelines for group participants?
Is there an advertising budget to promote the group?

Office for Science & Technology at the Embassy of France in the United States
Mission pour la Science et la Technologie de l'Ambassade de France aux Etats-Unis

Popolari

Frederic L.
Top Contributor

The Young Entrepreneurs initiative (YEi), started in 2005 and organized by The Office for Science and Technology at the Embassy of France in the US, is an accelerator designed to help ...

YEi 2014: Meet the Laureates feedproxy.google.com
The Young Entrepreneurs initiative (YEi), started in 2005 and organized by The Office for Science and Technology at the Embassy of France in the US, is an accelerator designed to help entrepreneurs grow their business in France and Europe. It provides an intensive training in Boston and Paris and a one week immersion in France that will allow laureates to benefit from an extensive customized busin

Consiglia (5) • Commenta (1) • Segui • 4 giorni fa

👍 Oscar C., Jacques B. e 3 altri utenti consigliano questo elemento

Sharon R. Bravo to all!
3 giorni fa

The LinkedIn group on Science and Technology created by the French embassy to the U.S.

CHAPTER 10
INSTAGRAM

Why use Instagram?

Instagram is a photo-video sharing platform that enables its users to take pictures and videos, apply digital filters and share them on a variety of social media, such as Facebook, Twitter or Tumblr.

A distinctive feature is that it confines photos to a square shape, similar to old Polaroid images, in contrast to the 4:3 aspect ratio typically used by mobile device cameras. Initially a purely photo-sharing service, in June 2013 Instagram incorporated video sharing, allowing its users to record videos lasting for up to 15 seconds.

Instagram was launched in October 2010 and was acquired by Facebook in April 2012 for approximately 1 billion dollars in cash and stock.

Some Instagram stats:
200 million active users worldwide.
An average of 60 million photos are posted every day.
41% of users are aged 16-24.
From December 2013 to May 2014 it has grown by 25%.

If you browse the pictures posted on Instagram, you will likely have the impression that this platform and its users have nothing to do with diplomacy or foreign policy. This is definitively a correct impression. However, Instagram is moving from a trendy app to a robust social network and, in fact, several governments and international leaders are trying to leverage its potential. I think that it would be worth at least pondering the possibility of including Instagram in your social media strategy for four main reasons:

1) You can use Instagram to engage your community and ask for user-generated content. Encouraging users to post their own photos with a call to action is an effective way to develop a community. If you work in an embassy, for instance, you might organize a contest on Instagram asking users to share images of their vacations in your country.

2) Instagram can be a powerful tool to connect with citizens. You can share behind-the-scene moments of international events, the whereabouts of Foreign Affairs ministers or ambassadors or just pleasant pictures that help "humanize" the diplomatic activity. It is important to understand that official photos of leaders shaking hands or diplomats speaking at conferences are unlikely to attract attention.

3) You can connect your Instagram account to other social media such as Facebook, Twitter, Foursquare, Tumblr and Flickr. When you link Instagram with your other channels, you'll easily be able to share content simultaneously on multiple networks. Plus, your followers on Facebook, Twitter, etc., will see that you are on Instagram and might follow you there too.

4) Rather than having just an institutional account on Instagram, it might also be valuable to encourage diplomats to run their own personal accounts where they can share images that bring audiences behind the scenes of their daily activity. This tactic is part of the major effort to establish an open and trustworthy relationship with your community, which is an essential requirement to disseminate your messages more effectively on social media.

The Instagram account of the British embassy to France

How to set up an Instagram account

You can download the Instagram app for iOS and Android, or view photos and follow users straight from the web. But you'll need to use the mobile app for uploading, editing, and sharing images as there's currently no way to do so from the official web platform.

After downloading the app, choose "Register with Email" to sign up with your email address. Create a username and password, fill out your profile info and then tap Done.

Your username on Instagram has to be recognizable, searchable and easy for your audience to remember. It is advisable to pick the same username your organization uses on other social networks and, possibly, to keep it short. Avoid words such as "instagram" or "ig", because they are often used by fake or spam accounts.

It's important to optimize your profile by adding a good description of your organization, which should be shorter than 150 characters, and your website address. You can even include a hashtag in your profile to showcase campaigns, events or contests you are promoting.

Once the description of your account is ready, you can upload your profile picture (recommended size is 110×110 pixels). Instagram profile pictures are rounded in the mobile app, and squared on the web. Therefore, choose a picture that will work with both formats. As you open your account, it is advisable to immediately share at least seven images, because the platform will automatically use them to create the big cover image on your profile. Since the cover is made of your most popular photos, it will continuously change and you cannot control it like on Facebook or Twitter.

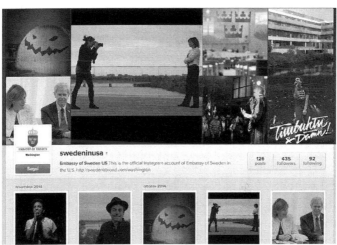

The Instagram account of the Swedish embassy to the U.S.

3 Web apps to enhance Instagram on desktop

The official Instagram web-based platform that allows you to manage the account from your desktop is very limited. Some third party developers filled in the gap, building excellent web-based apps that can help you manage your account more effectively. While there are tons of web apps available, the following ones are particularly noteworthy:

Iconosquare (formerly Statigram) lets you manage multiple Instagram accounts, browse your most important statistics, search for users and hashtags and monitor competitor and hashtag feeds.

Grid-Copygram allows you to browse photos of your own and other users in grid or list view with options to view in original size, follow other users, comment and like. There is the option to backup photos by downloading them to your computer too.

Gramfeed allows you to browse Instagram photos with links to users' profiles, with a follow button as well as comment and like options.

U.S. Ambassador to Thailand, Kristie Kenney, one of the most active diplomats on Instagram

10 tips to get the most out of Instagram

1) The standard size of Instagram photos is 612×612 pixels. It is advisable to make sure that all your photos look good in this size before sharing them.

2) Striking visual content grabs the attention of the users. Smartphone photos are good for in-the-moment action and instant uploads, but I recommend that you accurately edit your pictures and post only high-quality images.

3) Make it easy for users to find more information. If, for example, you post a picture of an event organized by your diplomatic mission, don't forget to include a link to your website with in-depth content about the event.

4) Don't just post informative photos, but try to be creative and share images that can create a special bond between users and your organization.

5) Adding hashtags in the caption of your photos is a great way to attract new followers and share your photos with more people. Use only specific and relevant hashtags and don't exceed 5-6 per photo.

6) In addition to providing your own imagery, ask users to share their images with you by using a particular hashtag. If you have a budget for prizes, you can also organize contests to engage your community and attract more followers.

7) "Regram" pictures. If you browse the platform, you will see that a lot of people take screenshots of pictures they like and then post them adding the tag "#regram". Regram fulfills the demand for a "sharing" feature that does not exist in the native Instagram app. Regramming is a good way to connect with people and there are third-party apps that allow you to reshare your favorite Instagram pictures.

8) To amplify your reach, you can embed an Instagram photo stream in your website or blog. This can show all of your pictures or just those tagged with a specific hashtag related to events or programs you are promoting.

9) Don't forget that Instagram also allows you to publish videos up to 15 seconds in length. Videos are popular, especially those of the behind-the-scenes variety, and can attract significant attention.

10) Learn to use third-party apps, like Iconosquare, to get detailed statistics on likes and followers of your account and to identify key influencers in your field.

ABOUT THE AUTHOR

Antonio Deruda is a communications consultant, trainer and speaker with 15 years of international experience.

He leads the digital team of a multinational brand and works with international organizations and governments to help them develop global online strategies. Prior to starting his consulting activities, Antonio worked as a media specialist for a U.S. embassy, where he had the opportunity to experience first-hand the impact of the digital diplomacy revolution.

He teaches postgraduate courses in digital diplomacy and international communication and offers custom-made training programs on digital diplomacy, social media marketing and crisis communication management for companies, international organizations and governments.

In 2012 he authored the book "Digital Diplomacy, Foreign Policy and Social Media", the first comprehensive study on this groundbreaking phenomenon.

When not online, Antonio loves to spend time with his family and ride his vintage motorcycle.

Made in the USA
Middletown, DE
12 October 2015